THE SONG OF THE

The Song of the Lord

A biblical guide to prophetic singing

TAMARA WINSLOW

KINGSWAY PUBLICATIONS

EASTBOURNE

ISBN 0 85476 509 3

Designed and produced by
Bookprint Creative Services
P.O. Box 827, BN21 3YJ, England, for
KINGSWAY PUBLICATIONS LTD
Lottbridge Drove, Eastbourne, E. Sussex BN23 6NT.
Printed in Great Britain.

To Michael, my husband and friend.
Your love, encouragement, support and friendship sustained me.
I couldn't have done this without you!

Contents

Preface

I can't remember a day when singing and loving God weren't a part of my life. Even at the young age of three I can recall sitting on my father's knee after an evening meal, or leaning alongside him in the truck as he drove along, with my little arm wrapped around his. All the while, the two of us would sing together, simply enjoying each other's company. As I grew up, my parents sacrificially invested countless hours of encouragement, tirelessly practising with me, taking me to those weekly vocal lessons, my mother accompanying me on the piano so that I could sing. For this I'll always be grateful. My parents wanted nothing but the best for me in developing the musical talent God had given me. It was in those young and formative years that God also called me into the ministry. I seldom spoke of what was in my heart, but burning deep within me was a hunger for his word, matched by a desire to share it through the power of his Spirit in preaching and in song.

My family were members of a small town Methodist church located in the farming area of the heartland of the United States. The people of that church were down-to-earth, almost isolated from the immensity of the world surrounding them. My public singing ministry began in that church. By the time I had reached the age of seven, I frequently sang solos. As I ministered the hymns and great songs of the church, a love and rock-solid foundation began to build as my heart embraced their message and power. Their words and melodies have been a vital factor in my spiritual growth. I'll always love those songs. They are my heritage and I find myself continually drawing from their wealthy treasure of truth as God stirs within me the new songs of the Spirit.

There is one experience of singing, though, that totally changed my life. At that time, God gave me my first insight into how the song of the believer is to be sung. I was somewhere between eight and eleven years old. It was Easter Sunday and I was scheduled to sing the old Easter favourite 'Were You There?'. I recall that while I was preparing to sing that Sunday morning, the reality of the song's text seemed to pierce my heart. I became acutely aware of the condition of the hearts of many of the people who would be present in the service, and of their need to know Jesus in a way they'd never known him before. I didn't really understand it, but I knew that I wanted to be able to sing in such a way that they would somehow meet him through the song. As the organist began to play, and I stood behind the micro-phone, I prayed a prayer that changed my life and my understanding of singing. The prayer was simple and childlike, but sincere. 'Lord Jesus, sing through me this morning, that the people might know you.'

Standing there, I looked towards the ceiling of the church, when suddenly the roof disappeared. Amazed, I saw descending from the heavens a lightning bright garment which fell on my shoulders. The power of God surged through me. I sang as I'd never sung before.

Now, years later, I understand from the Scriptures that what I'd prayed for was the anointing of the Spirit of God. It was my first experience with one of the types of the song of the Lord. I treasured this experience in my heart for many years before I ever shared it. But since that day, every time I have sung, I have prayed, asking Jesus to sing through me so that the people might know him. That's always been my heart's cry. Even in the teenage years of adjustment, I could never get away from this desire to sing his song. Throughout those years, I found myself composing numerous songs with one consistent theme. God began to develop the gift and to this day he's given me over 6,000 songs, with that number ever increasing as I yield myself to his song, his Spirit and his word.

Many years have passed since that first experience. Today, a dying world and a weary, passive church need his song more than they ever have before. Anointed, sanctified leaders and believing singers must awaken to be educated and learn to sing his song. The doors of hardened and sleepy hearts will once again be opened to encounter a glorified and risen Lord. The church has seen many counterfeits, all earnest attempts at this song. But Jesus will only be able to sing in and through his people when they sincerely embrace his word and Spirit. All other songs must be laid aside. His song demands the utmost commitment and faith. Born of the word and inspired by the Spirit, the song of the Lord issues forth from a heart unstained by pride and lust, and constantly renouncing the spirit of the world.

It is my earnest prayer that in this study many hearts will be released to sing God's song, his way. May a simple childlike prayer of faith be found on the lips of every servant of God desiring to hear his song for themselves. Then, as vessels filled with praise, we'll express that song to others, praying, 'Lord Jesus, sing through me so that they'll know you as they never have before.'

Introduction

> Repent therefore and be converted, that your sins may be blotted out, so that times of refreshing may come from the presence of the Lord, and that He may send Jesus Christ, who was preached to you before, whom heaven must receive until the times of restoration of all things, which God has spoken by the mouth of all His holy prophets since the world began (Acts 3:19–21).

The phrase 'times of restoration of all things' has always intrigued me. Any genuinely observant Christian, viewing the historical advancement of the church throughout the previous centuries, should be able to note the significant developments and spiritual renewals that have occurred. This present century has seen several distinct and progressive spiritual movements bringing about the restoration of some vital ingredients necessary to the maturing of the body of Christ. Such fundamental principles as healing, the baptism of the Holy Spirit and the ministry of the apostles and prophets have broken in upon the church scene once again, being first tolerated and then gradually fully embraced as the truth emerges from the shadows of many spiritually dark centuries. Each renewed principle contributes towards the fulfilment of the 'restoration of all things' as mentioned in Acts.

Considering these remarkable recoveries, and delighting in the prospect of those to come, I personally believe that soon the church is about to see the full restoration of the long-lost song of the Lord.

How does one define the term 'song of the Lord'? What distinguishes this song from others? Are there different types of this song? Are all spontaneous songs songs of the Lord? These are just a few of the many questions that need to be addressed concerning this vital subject.

It has always amazed me that so many leaders and believers alike are astonished when they realise that the song they have just heard sung in their midst, undeniably touching their heart, was spontaneously born for them, as a gift from Jesus. Some believers have a difficult time relating to the idea of something genuinely inspired, at the moment, by the Spirit. Bound by human reasoning, some well-meaning individuals unknowingly discard this form of new wine and seek a spirituality based solely on the intellect. There is also the other extreme. Christians, zealous to be used by God but lacking wisdom, spout off the first impressions that come to their mind. The distinction between the impulses of the individual human spirit and the gifts and unction of the Holy Spirit, fails to be noted. When this distinction isn't recognised, we may zealously minister solely from our good intentions, and sometimes even contradict the genuine ministry of God's Spirit. These feeble, often shallow efforts are frequently embraced as something spiritual, when in reality the songs are simply the individual's well-meaning heartfelt expression. We are in an extreme dilemma, but God's promises will prevail.

Where can we find understanding and help?

God's word teaches us very clearly about the song of the Lord. The first step is to define clearly what the song of the Lord is, and what it is not, by identifying the different types of song mentioned in the Scriptures, their stages of development and the various degrees of ministry. Our study must also include a review of secular and worldly songs in order to distinguish these from the songs belonging to God alone!

The phrase 'song of the Lord' is not common in the Scriptures and in fact occurs only in the Old Testament (though this does not exclude a New Testament ministry demonstration). Thus it is very difficult to define the phrase in simple terminology. The occasions on which it does occur in the Scriptures indicate that it's a very broad subject indeed. In fact the song of the Lord is identifiable in many forms, including all forms of praise and worship. For just a brief moment let us consider the songs which we will examine in depth later.

Old Testament manifestations of the song of the Lord

Undeniably, the most important type of the song of the Lord is the song which God himself sings. Therefore, when we speak of the song of the Lord, we must bear in mind that this is a song that first belongs to, and then proceeds from, the Lord God Almighty. His song is therefore *holy*. His songs express his deepest love. His songs also minister deliverance in times of trouble. This primary expression is fundamental to any growth in ministering the songs of the Lord.

Next, we shall examine songs of praise. This examination will be conducted in more depth than for some of the other categories since praise lays a vital foundation for singing the song of the Lord. We shall also investigate the new song and its spontaneous expression of praise; the prophetic song of witness; songs of prayer and supplication; songs of deliverance; and songs of joyful faith and triumph.

Finally, there is the song of the Lord given through spontaneous prophecy. This unusual expression seems to manifest in several forms such as praise, giving of thanks and prophecy. The words and melody would pour or bubble forth at a moment's notice. 'Prophecy', as translated from the Old Testament Hebrew, is defined as 'words which bubble forth in a spoken and a sung manner'. This point is very important when considering the New Testament perspective of this song of the Lord in prophecy.

New Testament manifestations of the song of the Lord

As believers we should glean understanding from the Old Testament forms of the song of the Lord, but we must also remember that we, as Christians, have received a new and better covenant. We must be careful neither to over-emphasise the Old Testament forms of praise and worship, nor to neglect the principles and lessons they contain. A balance of truth must be observed here if the song of the Lord is to be restored and released again in the church. What then are the expressions of the New Testament song of the Lord?

The New Testament expressions of the song of the Lord include a multiple category of songs identified as *spiritual songs*. These include singing with the spirit (better understood as singing in tongues), singing with the understanding, singing the interpretation of the tongues, prophecy, singing a word of knowledge, singing a word of wisdom and singing a new song. Each of these songs offers certain blessings and poses interesting problems to the growing believer.

Our New Testament search will also include an examination of the broad category of psalms and hymns.

As we study all the various examples mentioned in the Old and New Testaments we shall see that the song of the Lord has these characteristics: *it is born out of a right relationship with God and originates from his song as it is already real in the believer's heart; it is sung at the appropriate time and is led and anointed by the Spirit; it is often prophetic and prayer orientated; it may be either pre-written or spontaneous; it is scriptural; and it produces a deep and lasting effect on the heart of the participator and the listener.*

Successful ministry through God's songs involves embracing a dying world, while at the same time standing firm for purity and holiness. Just as he is holy, so is his song. When genuinely confronted with the anointing of God's Spirit, even the hardest-hearted unbeliever is touched and challenged to believe. In those precious moments, each soul is given a choice. I believe that God is searching for willing vessels who will mount up a guard for purity without religiosity. I believe he is yearning for some faith-filled saint to ask him for Spirit-born songs from his throne-room that bear a holy anointing, carry a powerful message, uncompromisingly speak the truth in love, and yet minister in such a way that anyone can identify with the message and understand it. I believe the time must come when God will anoint and raise up believers who will reject songs which are inspired by the spirit of this world and will long for genuine Holy Spirit-filled melodies which are able to convict both saint and sinner of truth. Then, finally, the song of the Lord will take its place as one of the tools that God will use in reaching lost souls in the Last Days.

Let us now take a look at the different types of song mentioned in the Bible so that we can gain wisdom discerning the genuine song of the Lord.

1

Understanding the Lord's Song

There were approximately 1,000 people present in the sanctuary that night. The praise and worship leaders had led the congregation into the presence of the Lord. As I stood there quietly worshipping, my heart was extremely restless. Like a warm and heavy garment, the anointing of God had come upon me during the worship time. My spirit felt as if it was about to explode. Over the years I'd become familiar with this inward wrestling. Even though I had only received two single words from the Lord, I instinctively knew a song from the Lord was about to be born. I discerned no melody, but I felt relieved to know at least what chord and key I was to play on the piano. Supplied with this bit of inspiration, I could start singing those two words. The Lord would give me the rest of the message. He'd always been faithful in doing so in the past. If I would be obedient in singing what I'd already received by faith, the words and music would come.

I suppose after over twenty years of singing and yielding to his promptings, one just begins to trust that he'll fill the mouth. This particular night was one of those special times, one of those anointed moments that make a mark upon the memory. After receiving acknowledgement from the pastor, I approached the piano, confident that

God was about to speak. Deliberately, in familiar surren-
der, my fingers moved across the keyboard and I began
singing. I felt the fermenting, explosive spiritual wine,
born within my human spirit. Words never before
uttered, in a melody never before sung, spontaneously
poured forth. The room became saturated with the
anointing of God. The song lasted for almost twenty
minutes. Suddenly, as the Spirit of God began to move
throughout the sanctuary, everyone unanimously,
without human prompting, fell to their knees, overwhelmed by the presence of an almighty God. Waves of
God's glory swept back and forth throughout the place. I
am sure that ranks of angels moved among the saints as
Jesus made himself known to his people. But the key to
this supernatural outpouring was something that has
been almost forgotten and even greatly misunderstood in
the church worldwide. That key is called the song of the
Lord.

Throughout the years, as I've travelled, I've consistently
been asked one particular question: 'How can *I* learn to
sing the song of the Lord?' It has become obvious to me
that church leaders and individual believers long to sing
the song of the Lord, but don't know how. There are many
Christians, in fact, who have never even known that such
a thing existed in God. The Judaean captives in Babylon
asked a very similar question: how can we sing the Lord's
song in a strange land? Judah's name is very significant in
understanding this question—it means 'praise'. Babylon's
name is also significant because it is defined as 'confusion'.
I'm continually amazed at the confusion that surrounds
praise and the song of the Lord. Even the definitions of
praise and worship are muddled and unclear, differing
with each person's interpretation. But thank God for the
truth of the word which will set us free.

Consider this: Jesus said that even though we live in this world, we are not of it. Our citizenship is in heaven. Therefore, we're strangers in a strange land. The tribe of Judah, captured by Babylon, was in the same predicament. Babylon attempted to force the Jews to sing the joyful songs of Zion; but we can make a choice to sing the song of the Lord because of our relationship with Jesus— there's no need for coercion. He's placed his song in our hearts and as we grow to know and love him, his song is one of the greatest opportunities for communion that we can participate in. Remember that the song of the Lord is like a seed. God is the originator of the song and as he sings to us, then seeds of praise, prayer, prophecy and worship are planted in our hearts. Our hearts are like gardens in which he sows the seeds of song. As we yield our hearts to him, those 'song seeds' will bear fruit, and a harvest of faithful, sensitive singing will be born.

God's song our model

If we're to learn how to sing the Lord's song, we'll need to acknowledge that his song can only be sung by those who have heard him sing it to them first. *His song is our model*. There are several scriptures that unveil the song he sings, supplying us with a pattern to follow. Jesus followed his Father's example, and so must we—and to do this we must further our relationship with him. The seed of the song is planted through this relationship. This is not too great a price to pay. Let's look at his song and find out what the patterns are.

Zephaniah 3 illustrates the song of the Lord in the most thorough fashion. To understand it we'll need to examine several Hebrew words that when translated into our language actually lose the intensity of their expression.

Sing, O daughter of Zion! Shout, O Israel! Be glad and rejoice with all your heart, O daughter of Jerusalem! The Lord has taken away your judgments, He has cast out your enemy. The King of Israel, the Lord, is in your midst; you shall see disaster no more. In that day it shall be said to Jerusalem: 'Do not fear; Zion, let not your hands be weak. The Lord your God in your midst, the Mighty One, will save; He will rejoice over you with gladness, He will quiet you with His love, He will rejoice over you with singing' (Zeph 3:14–17).

The Hebrew words used in this section of Scripture for 'singing' and 'sing' are *rinnah* and *ranan*. *Ranan* is the verbal root from which the noun *rinnah* comes. These words paint a dynamic picture of the first distinguishing characteristic of God's song. They refer to a song that sounds like a loud joyful cry of triumph. When God sings his song, he is totally uninhibited, extremely glad and bursting at the seams with absolute triumph. His song, which we are to imitate, even commanded to sing, is rarely quiet. Actually, it's the exact opposite. This is the type of song which he sings over his beloved, delivered people. But there's more!

His song is filled with rejoicing. Three different Hebrew words are used to express this. Verse 17 says, 'He will *rejoice* [*yasis*] over you with *gladness* [*simchah*].' These two words both convey the sense of bright, cheerful joy and gladness. Don't you wish that everyone in the body of Christ would imitate this quality in God's song? The third word is found at the end of verse 17; in the phrase '*rejoice* over you with singing' the verb used is *gil*, a word which describes one of the most radical expressions of joy in the Scriptures.

Gil means 'to turn and spin around in circles, as if under the influence of strong emotion'. This may surprise and even threaten the reserved individual. But consider this:

God is extremely moved by the intense love he has stirring in his heart for his people. His triumphant song is accompanied by a joyful dance resembling a whirlwind. He *is* emotional. He expresses his feelings with tremendous freedom and power as he sings. Why does the believer today resist and even resent such expressions when the pattern comes from God himself? Could there be two reasons? Are we wilfully disobedient to his word, and do we lack the depth of relationship with him that causes the song to be born? These are questions which we dare not ignore.

A challenge is presented in verse 14 of this passage. The daughter of Zion is *commanded* to sing in the same manner: the command '*Sing*, O daughter of Zion!' uses the verb *ranan*—the root of *rinnah*, the word which describes God's singing in verse 17. This song of the Lord, with all of its radical expressions of joy and triumph, is meant to be a corporate song of the Lord. Although the individual believer should be encouraged to flow in this, the congregation is commanded to. We as Christians have ample reason to sing such a song. God has given deliverance to his people. Jesus has triumphed over the works of the enemy. Have we become so numb and ungrateful that we don't even recognise it? Our frail human excuses must be laid aside and replaced by sincere obedience to his word, inspired by an ever-deepening relationship with him.

Almost all forms of praise mentioned in the Bible were demonstrated in an extreme and celebrative fashion. Praise can be defined as any form of singing, dancing, lifting of hands, shouting, clapping, leaping and rejoicing that expresses thankfulness for what God has done in the past and for what he will do as if it's already done. Praise is essentially faith in action. Worship, however, is defined as any form of singing or physical demonstration exhibited with humility and love to honour God for who he is. Worship, in its truest form, was ministered as the worshipper lay prostrate before the Lord. It is essentially love in action. Worship, the quieter expression of the song of the Lord, is almost entirely reserved for the individual or small group. It demands an intimacy difficult to express in a large group setting.

How can we hear his song and then imitate it? When does his song come to us? What is the purpose of his song and what does it result in, for the believer?

In Zephaniah 3:15 and 17, a wonderful revelation unfolds: the Lord lives in the midst of us, and is mighty. You are God's dwelling place, his temple, a residence for his presence. Until you treasure that relationship and deem his presence more valuable than any other thing, you'll not experience the full freedom of his song.

His song reminds you of his victory. It always lifts you up in encouragement, triumph and faith. He believes in his people far more than they may know or believe in the One who indwells them. Greater is he that is in us, than the enemy we face in the world. His song reminds us of this inheritance. We have great cause to sing!

God's song is born in times of trouble

David understood some things about God's song that we need to learn.

David was a man of incredible depth. He was also a man who walked alone. He faced adverse circumstances, experienced the rejection of trusted friends, endured long years of awaiting his destined calling and tasted the bitterness of carnality. Yet in the midst of his darkest hours, some of his greatest songs of triumph and praise were born. David was a man who had learned to listen to God's song and he overcame the circumstances oppressing him by the use of praise.

> O my God, my soul is cast down within me; therefore I will remember You from the land of the Jordan, and from the heights of Hermon, from the Hill Mizar. Deep calls unto deep at the noise of Your waterfalls; all Your waves and billows have gone over me. The Lord will command His lovingkindness in the daytime, and in the night His song shall be with me—a prayer to the God of my life (Ps 42: 6–8).

According to Psalm 42, it was in the night that David heard God's song. Night signifies a difficult hour of adversity, but it also signifies a time for deliverance. At a time when David felt overwhelmed, he chose to listen to the songs of the Lord instead of the songs of discouragement and doubt. God's song here was also mixed with David's prayer. When his heart thirsted for God's presence, this song came. (The Hebrew word for 'song' in this psalm is *shir*, the word most commonly used for the song of the Lord in the Old Testament.)

David often experienced trouble and distress as is evident from the numerous psalms which he composed at such times. Another example is found in Psalm 32:

> For this cause everyone who is godly shall pray to You in a time when You may be found; surely in a flood of great waters they shall not come near him. You are my hiding place; You shall preserve me from trouble; You shall surround me with songs of deliverance (Ps 32:6–7).

In an hour when the floods of life seemed about to close in on him, David knew to hide in the secret place of the

Most High, where he found a refuge of protection. In that covering presence he would hear the Lord's song of deliverance, surrounding him on every side, building a faith-filled rampart of hope and safety. There in that secret place God uses his song to remind us that he will fight for us as we humbly hide ourselves in his presence.

The song of the Lord is heard in the secret place

The Lord's song of deliverance is found only in that secret place. I want to emphasise that it is *not* a quiet song. It is a song of triumph and freedom. The Hebrew word for 'song' in 'songs of deliverance' (Ps 32:7) is *ron*, which is related to *ranan* and *rinnah*. When the Lord sings that song to the hiding believer, he gives instruction to the confused and fearful heart, releasing his tender mercy towards the afflicted soul. It's no wonder David said that he rejoiced when he was hidden under the shadow of the wings of the Almighty.

Nothing can replace the safety found in the secret place of the Most High. No human relationship will ever truly calm the battle-weary heart like the relationship with the Lord and his ministry of song. There, we are protected from words of strife and division. There, the plots of wickedness fail and the pride of man is diverted away. Yet as Christians wander further and further away from his presence, trusting in quick answers founded upon man's wisdom, God's song of deliverance becomes but a faint whisper, fading into the distance. In fact, few have ever heard that song. Don't you think it's time to take our refuge in him and listen to him as he sings the songs of deliverance to a needy people?

Countless individuals have approached me and told me how they desire to sing the songs of deliverance to others. Yet frequently I find that they themselves are in grave need of deliverance from God. They have never learned to rest in his arms and listen to his songs of deliverance to them personally. How can they be fit to minister to others when they are also bound? We must learn to hear his song for ourselves first. Then, as we can be trusted to share his song with others, he will plant those 'song seeds' in our heart. Without this source of inspiration, we are like the blind leading the blind.

I believe we can truly echo the cry of the Judaean captives and say, 'How shall we sing the Lord's song in a strange land?' The Scriptures are clear. He has given us some wonderful guidelines. Now it is up to us to follow them.

2

Secular Songs in Scripture

There are many different types of song mentioned in the Scriptures and each one is significant, emphasising a different purpose and producing a unique result. It is essential that we understand this if we are to minister wisely the type of song that God wants to use to meet a particular spiritual need.

Ignoring the scriptural truths God has established in his word results in an unhealthy over-emphasis on the experiences of the Spirit and the gifts of the Spirit. Such an attitude is surely spiritually immature. Embracing the necessary biblical truths and principles is a fundamental step towards restoring the song of the Lord which, without this revelation, becomes shallow, emotionally based and lacking in genuine spirituality.

Singing and music played a very important role in the personal, corporate, secular and spiritual expressions throughout the entire Bible. Although there were no radios, cassette tapes or music recordings, songs of all types were developed, sung, shared and even became popular among the people. It wasn't uncommon to see groups of strolling minstrels singing the popular songs of the day. They communicated the important events of the times and were very much like a musical walking newspaper. New songs travelled quickly from one area of the country to another. These songs were sung by both men and women and became a very important means of expression to the society of that day.

Let us consider the various types of secular song mentioned. This will enable us to distinguish worldly songs from those which originate from the Lord.

Songs used to send people on their journeys

The first mention of a song is found in Genesis 31:27. It occurred in a situation similar to the modern-day custom of a 'going away party'. Laban tells Jacob that he would have sent him on his way with songs of joy, had Jacob not stolen away secretly. It would seem that this was the usual custom of the day.

Songs used in idol worship

Singing was also used for the worship of idols. Following the direction of pagan priests, the people sang by course, repeating every phrase, as they submitted themselves to vile and immoral acts. The song was frenzied and extremely forceful and was sung while going through the motions of browbeating, eventually abasing the singer into an utterly worthless state of being. Such a song is utterly alien to the nature of God and directly opposes the true song of the Lord.

One might suppose that a Christian believer could never sing such a song—but this may not necessarily be the case. Occasionally, in times of revival or intense expressions of music ministry, the focus of the song is lost and results in something entirely carnal. The true song of the Lord may be energetic, loud, forceful and rhythmical, but it never exchanges humility for worthless self-abasement; rhythm for uncontrolled, frenzied actions; volume for abrasive, confused sound; joy for self-indulgence. This type of ungodly song is built on the leader's emotional hype and driving momentum. Woe to the believer who follows a leader who worships the beauty of the song instead of the beauty of the Lord. That is a form of idolatry of which the church must beware!

Idolatrous songs in the church

The scene which Exodus 32 describes produced the type of demonic singing mentioned in the previous paragraph. Moses had been absent for an unusually long time. The people became restless and eventually persuaded Aaron to construct an idol in the shape of a golden calf. They had quickly forgotten the Lord God and wilfully involved themselves in a heated and idolatrous form of worship. Please note that even Joshua didn't discern the true nature of this type of singing (v 17). Only Moses saw through the spiritual charade. Even the most sincere heart can be blinded and caught up in the emotional hype of such singing. Defiling the individual, it eventually brings death upon all who participate. The body of Christ needs Moses-type leaders to arise and expose the fallacy of this song.

Songs of the travelling minstrels

A third type of song mentioned in the Bible has already been mentioned briefly. Minstrels, singing men and women who travelled in groups, singing and dancing to the accompaniment of various rhythm instruments, would sing many different types of song.

'Musical newspapers'

Some of the minstrels' songs reported significant events of the time. For example, they would welcome kings and soldiers returning from the battlefield with songs of honour announcing their victories.

Short and simple, this song possessed a catchy tune. Quickly learned and committed to memory, the song spread rapidly across the land. In some cases, this type of song could pose a problem. King Saul, home from the battlefield, enjoyed the praise of the singers as they recounted his victories in combat. But when he heard them extolling the victories of the young triumphant David more than his own, Saul was consumed by rage and jealousy, and plotted David's death from that fateful day. Wherever he went, this song followed David. It constantly stirred up the leaders against him, or caused suspicion. (See 1 Samuel 18:6–9; 21:10–12; 29:5.) Such songs don't always have a happy ending.

The minstrels' songs of entertainment and refreshment

These singing men and women also provided much of the musical entertainment of the era. Their songs were sung to soothe kings, like troubled King Saul. They entertained the people and refreshed the leaders. Solomon even gathered these singers for his personal entertainment and pleasure (Eccles 2:7–9).

Modern society is filled with such singing. Like the fluctuating temperature, singing groups of numerous and varied styles rise and fall. All of their songs, no matter what method they use, fail to fill the void in the heart of man that only God's song can satisfy. Solomon, considering all he had done in gathering singers and songs around him, was overwhelmed by the futility of a man's life. The songs of man, without God, are empty: 'Then I looked on all the works that my hands had done and on the labor in which I had toiled; and indeed all was vanity and grasping for the wind. There was no profit under the sun. Then I turned myself to consider wisdom and madness and folly; for what can the man do who succeeds the king?— Only what he has already done' (Eccles 2:11–12).

Singers sang to honour kings. Singers sang to mourn over the death of leaders in lamentation. They sang as they worked in the vineyards during harvest. They sang under the influence of alcohol. These singers even sang to mock the people of God and godly leaders.

The minstrels' songs of mockery

Jeremiah the prophet was mocked by such singing (Lam 3:14). The song was repeated all day long and known by a large portion of society. This mocking song is intended to silence the prophet, attempting to sow the seeds of bitterness in the soul of the prophetic ministry. Yet it did not stop the word of the Lord through Jeremiah.

David also experienced such negative publicity and singing. Those who were drunken and mocking sang against him: 'Those who sit in the gate speak against me, and I am the song of the drunkards' (Ps 69:12).

Job called these songs of mockery a song of fools: 'They were sons of fools, yes, sons of vile men; they were scourged from the land. "And now I am their taunting song; yes, I am their byword. They abhor me, they keep far from me; they do not hesitate to spit in my face"' (Job 30:8–10).

No one understood Job's condition. Even his closest friends misjudged him. No one understood David or Jeremiah. The songs which were sung against these faithful men of God were based not on knowledge of the truth but on opinion. Why does man listen to such singing? Yet this type of song is common today. Thousands of lyrics and melodies are composed out of personal opinions and judgements. Born of ignorance and pride, these songs destroy lives; but those who write them give no thought to the consequences. Man is notorious for singing songs about things he doesn't understand.

This is why it is so very important that when the song of the Lord is composed, it should originate from the truth of the Scriptures, the love of God and *all the facts*.

The songs of prostitution and harlotry

Singers even sang for the ungodly purpose of harlotry. The prostitutes of the day, in order to allure their victims, would flagrantly sing a song of wantonness, seducing even the most innocent. Each prostitute was known for the song she sang as she looked for someone to trap in her deathly snare.

The songs of the ancient city of Tyre are compared to the song of a prostitute, attempting to entice the listener into fleshly sin for the purpose of monetary gain and economic trade. Of course it has an all-too-familiar ring in today's society where countless thousands of dollars are spent each year on the type of songs that the modern world knows as advertisements. These songs sell a product, attracting prospective buyers. Their melodies are deceitfully sweet, pleasant to listen to and easy to remember. Tyre is still singing its harlot's song, attempting to seduce eager, unsuspecting listeners to purchase its merchandise. None the less, God will accomplish his will in this last hour. The merchandise and hire of Tyre will end up being a blessing to the kingdom of God. God will take the song that the world wants to use for its own gain, and cause it to be a blessing to his kingdom (see Isaiah 23:16–18). How this will be accomplished is entirely up to the Lord, but it will definitely be a wonder to see it fulfilled.

The songs of Babylon

This is the last type of secular song, and probably the most important.

Babylon was once a great capital city of the Chaldean empire, located in present-day Iraq and ruled by some of the most idolatrous, wicked kings ever to reign in the earth. It was a major economic and religious centre of the ancient world and it also became a centre for music. Babylon is known as the Great Harlot, the Mother of Harlots. Therefore, its song will be seductive and enticing to the flesh.

According to the Scriptures, Babylon was filled with music. During the days of Daniel, King Nebuchadnezzar reigned in the city of Babylon; vain and desiring the praises of men, he constructed a golden statue in his own likeness. Whenever the people of Babylon heard the sound of a certain type of music, they were expected to fall down and worship the golden image. Those who refused would suffer the penalty of death in a fiery furnace.

Three Hebrews, Shadrach, Meshach and Abednego, refused to bow down and respond to this ungodly song because of their faith and commitment to God. These three men didn't fear the fires of King Nebuchadnezzar. They feared their God. Even when cast into a fiery furnace which Nebuchadnezzar had decreed to be seven times hotter than usual, they were protected and delivered by God's hand. Their miraculous deliverance stunned the king and resulted in a powerful victory.

The Islamic call to prayer is a modern type of this idolatrous, commanding song. The enemy's songs are still the same.

Babylon isn't just an enemy or city of the past. It is a religious and economic system ruling much of the world today. The Scriptures indicate that this great harlot will be judged in the last days and all that is within it will fall, *even its songs and music* (see Revelation 18:21–22).

Could many Christians unknowingly yield to the songs of the harlot, bowing to the idols of money, lust, immorality, adultery, false religions and selfishness, loving the world more than they fear God? Like a recording that constantly repeats itself, the songs of the harlot can entrap the soul if they are not determinedly refused. The words and melody are hauntingly seductive, but not impossible to defeat. Unless the believer refuses to respond to this song, the believer will fall.

Babylon as an idolatrous religion

Babylon's songs mock everything that is holy about the song of the Lord. While the song of the Lord is born out of a love for God, Babylon's songs are born out of a love for self. When the song of the Lord calls for trust and dependence on God, the songs of Babylon promote a false sense of prosperity and independence. Since Babylon is a habitation for devils (Rev 18:2) the songs of Babylon are, for the most part, demonically inspired. The song of the Lord is inspired through fellowship with God. The songs of Babylon, created for soulish and fleshly entertainment, appeal to the senses, the emotions and the mind, ignoring the condition of the spirit of man. These songs will never satisfy the spiritual hunger for God that only the song of the Lord can express. Babylon's songs deny the personal responsibility one has for one's life, casting blame on everyone else for one's own mistakes. The songs of Babylon make merchandise of other men's souls, enslaving them in the clutches of the spirit of the world.

This present-day enemy, the composer of this ungodly song, has captured unwary Christians. Compromise has replaced the sincere heart of commitment. Babylon is a system that keeps its victims living in a state of subtle bondage without extreme oppression, unless they rebel against its system of idolatry. Historically, Babylon was the conqueror of the tribe of Judah. During the years of Babylonian captivity, most of the Jews were allowed to live as they desired. They built houses, planted gardens and were encouraged to put down roots. In that period they lost much of their language; they began to obey the verbal interpretations of the word of God given by the priests and became followers of an oral law, thereby laying aside the heart of faith. Eventually, the identity and the culture of Babylon became part of them by a gradual and subtle process which posed no direct threat to their existence and gave the illusion of freedom. Today's form of Babylon may not seem to present any real threat to the song of the Lord and the church, but we must beware of being subtly seduced into thinking that it's acceptable to adopt the songs of Babylon and compromise in an attempt to fit into the world. That old battle is still raging.

Babylon as an economic system

We have seen that Judah's name means 'praise'. Is it coincidental that Babylon captured the tribe of praise? Could it be that the Babylon of today has captured true praise and the song of the Lord? Babylon wanted to hear the Judaean captives sing the songs of Zion (Ps 137:3). This interest in the song of the Lord still persists and is inspired by the desire for monetary gain; Babylon is an economic as well as a religious system. Babylon has made many attempts to imitate and merchandise the song of the Lord and thus to defile it, mocking God. But the song of the Lord cannot be bought and sold; nor will Babylon ever be able to duplicate it successfully. The song of the Lord can come only from a heart sold out to Jesus; and it produces eternal results, bringing peace to the weary soul, joy to the heavy heart and deliverance to those in bondage to sin and death.

What are the implications of all of this for Christian music now? Has the insidious infiltration of Babylon, which I have been describing, affected all contemporary Christian music? I think it would be wrong to make generalisations about this. But if in fact we do form a negative judgement about a particular song, a further question arises. Jesus said that a tree's nature can be known by the fruit it produces. In judging against a song, are we then condemning its composer? I don't feel that it is my responsibility to judge the heart of any Christian songwriter; nor do I know any of them well enough to do so. I do believe that it is important to maintain godly standards in music and that we should not unthinkingly accept any song which appears—but as far as the condition of the heart is concerned our prime responsibility is to maintain godly standards in our own hearts.

It may be that there are some Christian singers and composers who have been seduced by Babylon and who have ungodly motives. But prayer, patience and love will defeat the enemy's work far more effectively than condemnation and possibly wrong judgements. I am aware that my judgement of certain songs may be influenced by my personal preferences in music and by my own religious and cultural background. Also, I'm still

growing and making mistakes myself, so I don't feel qual-
ified to pass judgement on others. Only God knows what
is in another person's heart.

Finally, the song of the Lord is a concept almost
unheard of in the church today. Could it be that Babylon
has swallowed up the truth of the song and a shallow
counterfeit has replaced it? Whatever the reasons, a stern
cry will soon be lifted from heaven's throne. It is time for
God's people to come out of Babylon and for Babylon to
come out of them (Rev 18:4–6). We must examine the
motives of our hearts, and the seductive songs of Babylon
must be laid aside. God has a song to give and a message
to sing in the earth that will shake the nations before Jesus
returns. It will be a pure song, one unrestrained by the
fear of man, religious traditions, fiery furnace or love of
money. That song cannot be sung in Babylon's confusion.
It must be sung in truthful remembrance of what Jesus
accomplished on the cross.

It is time to recognise the threat that this harlot represents to the song of the Lord. God's people must awake
from deception and counter Babylon's evil work with
double power-packed resolve and force. Let this be a challenge! Take up your harp again, church, and sing the song
of the Lord. Don't shrink back any longer!

3

His Song in Praise: The Corporate Song

Several years ago, my husband Michael and I were driving to a friend's house to attend a dinner party. Michael had tuned in to a local Christian radio station playing Christian music. The old hymn 'Crown him with many crowns' was being played. I was enjoying this beautiful piece, sung magnificently by a massive choir in a musical arrangement such as I'd never heard before and I wasn't in the least prepared for what was about to happen. Suddenly, as if caught away into a dream, I found myself standing in a huge pavilion that went as far as my eye could see. As I beheld this marvel, I was stunned by the multitudes of people filling the place. It appeared as if a sea of human faces went on and on in every direction. Then, as if given some silent signal, this mass of humanity began to sing. Their unified voices sounded like the rolling, thunderous ocean waves pounding the seashore. The song caused the very atmosphere to pulsate with each distinct word and note. Overcome with a sense of wonder, I suddenly realised where I was as the people began to sing 'Worthy is the Lamb that was slain'. But more important still, I recognised when it was. It was the first moment that all who had ever known Jesus Christ as their Lord and

Saviour were gathered together in the heavenly family before the throne of God. It was the first time they had ever sung that song in perfect unity of faith. As I stood there, it suddenly occurred to me why this song sounded so different. Never before had I heard God's people sing without pride affecting their song. Never before had I heard God's people sing without someone attempting to 'out sing' the others. Never before had I heard the song of the heart so unpolluted and clean. At the same time I became acutely aware of the oneness of the song, even though it was totally unrehearsed. Still, in such a mass of people, not one person felt ignored. The Lord lovingly knew each heart as if each person stood singing there alone.

It all was happening so quickly, and as I turned to see who was standing next to me in this congregation of saints, I suddenly found myself back in the car. I have to admit it was quite a let down. But then the Lord spoke something to me that I will never forget. He said, 'The body of Christ must begin to prepare for that day when they shall gather together as one and sing before me with one voice.'

Our ultimate destiny is to join with the crowd around the throne and sing praise to the Lord. If we are to prepare ourselves for that day we must begin now to learn to praise him. This is the first necessity in singing the song of the Lord. We must first have a right relationship with God, expressed in praise, before we attempt to sing the song of the Lord for any other purpose—for ministry or prophecy, for example. Such attempts, without a prior commitment to praise, are empty and selfish.

Perhaps we can gain some insight into this by looking briefly at the Hebrew words most commonly used in the Old Testament to signify song; that is, the verb *shir* and its derivatives. The references in which words of this group occur tell us two things. The first is that there is a wide variety of songs of the Lord: these words are used of songs of praise, songs of testimony, psalms, new songs, songs of witness, songs of ministry and prophetic songs. But the second thing to note is that, significantly, the biggest category is songs of praise to God; we shall consider some of these in this chapter.

In view of the pre-eminence of praise we shall examine these songs in more detail than some of the other types of song; in so doing we shall have a solid basis from which to consider other aspects of the song.

As we consider the songs of praise, we must remember that the first step is to hear the song which God sings to the listening believer. His song, like a seed, takes root in the believer's heart and if it is nurtured by prayer, the word and an ongoing relationship with God it will germinate and produce other songs. Secondly, continued growth will depend on these songs of the Lord in praise being practised within the context of a disciplined lifestyle. These two principles form the solid foundation which is essential if there is to be an anointing on his song; and they apply not only to songs of praise but also to all other types of the song of the Lord.

Songs of the Lord in praise may be either corporate or individual. I will examine the corporate song in this chapter and in the next chapter I will look at the individual song.

Corporate praise in the songs of the Lord was never quiet. Most of the time it was extremely loud, mixed with shouting and joyful celebration and accompanied by a wide variety of instruments, including trumpets, timbrels, harps and psalteries. Remember that God's song was sung to the saints in a similar manner as mentioned in Zephaniah 3:17. The pattern is consistent throughout the Scriptures.

In the spirit of might

The first point concerning the corporate song of praise is that it is done in the unction of the spirit of might. This is how David and all Israel played and sang to God as they were transporting the Ark of the Covenant.

If the body of Christ were to sing God's song in praise in the way which the Scriptures consistently reveal, the spirit of heaviness wouldn't be able to enter the church doors. The attitudes that restrict this type of the song of the Lord in praise are predominantly rooted in fear and our sophisticated approach to Christianity. But the benefits of releasing such praise far outweigh these considerations. God's glory cloud manifests when the corporate song of praise is released; he fights for his people and defeats their enemies. But fear not! God will have a people who will praise him unashamedly before he returns. The song of exuberant, corporate praise will be restored and it will shatter the self-righteous, legalistic, man-fearing icons that the church has erected throughout history.

To the Lord

Secondly, this corporate song of praise was sung directly *unto the Lord*. One of the greatest weaknesses I have observed in praise today is the superficial attitude with which we address God in praise. This is a result of a lukewarm relationship that must be challenged if we're to grow. One can never sing unto the Lord if one has little or no relationship with him. The Book of Revelation is very clear about God's feelings to those who are lukewarm. He vomits them out. If our songs of the Lord are not sung with fervent faith, love and intense will they are not worthy of being offered to him. Perhaps this is one of the reasons why the tangible manifestation of the glory of the Lord comes so seldom in the church. The corporate song of the Lord in praise is directed to him. The purpose of entertainment has no place in his song.

A godly order

Thirdly, the corporate song of the Lord in praise was to be practised in a manner consistent with the requirements of God and in an orderly manner. ('Orderly', however, does not mean 'quiet'.) This order is seen again and again throughout the Old Testament. David, for example, instructed the Levitical leaders to appoint certain individuals to play the ordained instruments and sing specific types of songs of thanksgiving and praise. David learned the importance of such an order the hard way. David's intentions in the first relocation of the Ark were good, but they weren't according to God's instructions and as a result Uzza perished. Even though we may possess good intentions, we still recklessly steam ahead in praise. We may eventually reach our goal, but how much fruit and how many lives are sacrificed along the way simply because we didn't seek to discover God's order before we started out?

Another characteristic of the corporate song of the Lord in praise is the existence of a proper authority structure. David, Asaph, Heman, Juduthun, Hezekiah and other leaders were responsible for giving specific oversight to the song. These leaders received from God the vision and direction in which the praise was to be ministered and then instructed the actual praise leaders. The directions contained in these visions were then established as foundational principles, defining how the corporate song of praise should be sung; this was usually done on the authority either of kings or those who functioned in the prophetic ministry. David was a prophet, as stated in Acts 2:29–30. Asaph, Heman and Jeduthun were seers—another name for prophet. Others, such as Nathan and Gad, also gave commands and set boundaries of operation and expectation for those who would lead the songs of the Lord in corporate praise. This oversight and prophetic foundation is essential. Without it, the corporate song of the Lord becomes legalistic, empty of spiritual depth and confused and the way is open for chaos, criticism and the flesh.

Boundaries and expectations derived from godly vision are necessary and practical, but they frighten individualistic believers. A desire for liberty of the Spirit should never override the practical application of the word of God. Attitudes such as this promote freedom without wisdom, resulting in selfish manifestations of God's songs for merely personal edification and fulfilment. The order and principles God gave to David and the prophets will apply and work in today's church.

A unified manner

Next, the corporate song of the Lord in praise is expressed in a unified manner. There can't be enough said about the importance of this quality. In an attempt to present a beautiful sound, singleness of heart and voice is frequently deemed unimportant. Please don't misunderstand me here. Harmony, beautiful arrangements and variety of presentation definitely have a place in praise.

These elements, however, can never be a substitute for the power that is released when human voices unite in one single note and heart. Scientifically, such a sound pierces the atmosphere like a mighty spear. If it is sung in faith and joy and with a unified will, such a song becomes a mighty tool in the hand of the Lord and brings glory to God.

The corporate song of the Lord in praise entitled the 'new song'

The subject of prophetic song will be considered in detail later. But let's notice here that the song of the Lord in praise has a vital prophetic dimension: the corporate song of the Lord in praise sometimes emerges in a form called the new song (*shir chadash*: *chadash* means new, fresh or recent).

There are several points to be made concerning the new song. A number of the Psalms refer to it: 33:3; 40:3; 96:1; 98:1; 144:9; 149:1. In nearly every instance the context is one of rejoicing for God's deliverance in time of trouble. Frequently the song was accompanied by a variety of instruments—harps, horns, trumpets, timbrels—and sometimes by shouts of joy. It is a song full of celebration.

But what makes this new song so special is that it is born out of a fresh and exciting revelation of God's delivering power. The words to a new song were not previously composed; they are newly born out of the womb of the joyful heart. This song is created in an atmosphere where the believer enjoys an invigorating relationship with God. Do you enjoy your relationship with him? The Christian who sings a new song is thrilled with him!

Perhaps the new song can also be ministered using old words with a fresh zeal. But however that may be, the new song is a song that is born because of joyful reflection on the delivering and mighty hand of the Lord.

Psalm 149 indicates that this new song of praise, when sung in the congregation of the saints, may also *result* in a powerful demonstration of God's deliverance, binding the enemy with chains that cannot be broken and executing God's judgement on our foes. Isaiah 42:10–13 reveals a similar result. It seems that when the saints of God enter into a new song of praise, this opens the doors for God to go forth into battle for us against our enemies. It is also quite possible that this new song may be what we understand to be high praise.

This song requires more faith and dependence on God than any other, because generally the words have never been sung before. Leaders must be extremely sensitive to lead it accurately. The hearts of the congregation must be in unity and joyful submission in order to follow and flow together without competition. God must receive the glory entirely. What tremendous possibilities it holds for those who are yielded and walking in love and faith!

I personally believe that in the days before the return of Christ, we shall also see a return of this type of song.

In the summer of 1989, I was speaking at a youth conference in the heartland of the United States. One evening, during the praise and worship service, the words for a new song began to stir with great intensity within my spirit. I waited for an opening and then signalled to one of the leaders that I had a song. As the song began, it came with tremendous force and before I knew it we were 'caught up' into the presence of the Lord. The words for a simple chorus of praise began to emerge. In that moment, several hundred young people joined me in this prophetic song. Together we sang this new song of praise to the Lord for ten to fifteen minutes. The song made a mark on the hearts of everyone present, one which remains even now, several years later. It also continues to inspire those who hear it for the first time. This new song was like fresh water to tired hearts. It encouraged and lifted those who were weary, and stirred their hearts to praise God in a united and prophetic manner.

This type of fresh, new song expresses the joy of those who have seen God's deliverance and encourages those who are weary. It will be heard again in the land and the powers of darkness can't stop it!

4

His Song in Praise: The Individual Song

The individual expression of praise in the song of the Lord is not always as loud and exuberant as the corporate song of the Lord. It can be set to enthusiastic music or it may be gentle and sweet. Most of the time it is moderate in volume and style. It was either accompanied by stringed instruments or done *a cappella*. The individual song of the Lord in praise is primarily created to be used in personal devotions.

The key to unlocking the power of this type of song is in the focus of the heartfelt words. It must be sung *to* the Lord. This requires a commitment of the heart, not a feeling. Waiting for the necessary emotional feeling before singing unto the Lord can be a futile business. Seldom do the emotions provide the initial motivation for praise. Moses, David and Deborah, all prophetic ministers, made a deliberate choice to praise, not relying upon their feelings alone, and we can follow their example. This requires a discipline of thought, emotion and will but if one is willing to reflect upon the past works of the Lord, both faith and praise will begin to stir in the heart. Deborah, a prophetess and judge, reflected on the victory over Sisera and as a result composed a magnificent poem which was a mighty song of praise to the Lord.

The individual song of the Lord in a new song

Occasionally a song of the Lord will be born in an individual's devotional life which is described as the new song.

The individual new song takes many forms and is ministered according to the circumstances and atmosphere surrounding it. It may sometimes happen that a person who lacks a daily devotional time will attempt to remedy this lack by ministering such a song in the group setting. For example, a Christian struggling with feelings of rejection may do this in order to increase his self-esteem and appear spiritually wise. It is wrong to use the corporate gathering to meet personal needs which should be met in private prayer. When God uses the song, everyone is edified. When David spoke of the new song in Psalms 40:3 and 144:9, he defined it as praise unto God. It is obvious that he sang this in his private time with the Lord long before he ever ministered it publicly. It was a song of testimony and victorious breakthrough.

Secondly, David's new songs emerged out of the difficult circumstances of life. Again a thankful, disciplined heart of faith is the seed bed for the new song.

Thirdly, he stated that God had put the words in his mouth; for this to be so, he must have spent time in the presence of the Lord. This cannot be ignored, but often is.

Next, this new song proved to be a tool to reach those who do not know God. If sung with the right heart and to the Lord, this song, ministered under a fresh anointing, will cause unbelievers to be drawn to him and also soften the heart of the backslider. It is one of the most powerful evangelistic tools available to the Christian musician. The conditions for ministering this song are quite clear. The believer who has received such a song must trust the Lord implicitly, not being moved by fear of man. This song, although it has a prophetic aspect, is different from other prophetic songs in that it is specifically a song of praise to God. Prophetic songs, as you will see later, have a much wider field of expression.

New songs born for prophetic times through individuals

Occasionally an individual may receive a new song that is only to be sung at a specific and prophetic time. Isaiah gives an example: '*In that day this song will be sung* in the land of Judah: "We have a strong city; God will appoint salvation for walls and bulwarks. Open the gates, that the righteous nation which keeps the truth may enter in"' (Is 26:1–2). It seems that each new dispensation of God in the earth throughout history has its own song. This type of song involves declaration. God bears witness in the hearts of all his people that it is time for this song to be sung. No one can force this song. It only erupts at certain prophetic times. It is not a common manifestation, but we need to know that this type of song exists.

The possibility of misinterpretation of prophetic songs

As we will consider later, the prophets were most probably very adept at flowing in the song of the Lord. This is not to imply that every prophecy was sung, but the definition of the Hebrew word for prophecy strongly indicates that many prophecies could have been sung. There is one particular time and one particular prophet, though, that we need to consider at this point.

In Ezekiel 33:31–33, God refers to Ezekiel as a man gifted in singing the songs of the Lord in a prophetic sense. Ezekiel also faced a problem. He was called to deliver a word which he knew the people would fail to believe even though, as the Scriptures suggest, God had gifted him with the ability to sing that prophecy in a gentle, tender and beautiful manner. The people deemed his prophetic word in song to be a song designed for their entertainment. Only after this word was fulfilled would the people understand that they had indeed heard the voice of a prophet.

How frequently has this misinterpretation occurred in the church today? If God were to minister a genuine prophetic word through song, a great number of churches wouldn't even know what had happened. They might quietly and appreciatively applaud the entertainment, but not realise until much later what had occurred. I believe one reason this is so is because there have been so many counterfeits. I am praying that the need for the genuine song of the Lord will be clearly recognised within the body of Christ.

5

Songs of Ascents and Songs of Witness

In this chapter we will look briefly at two more types of song which fall into the *shir* category.

Songs of ascents

Have you ever noticed that when the heart of a congregation is in agreement, then the songs of praise create a spiritual staircase ascending gradually upwards into the realm of the Spirit? And that when there is discord and complex, difficult songs of praise, the things of the Spirit are stifled?

The psalmist, in Psalms 120 to 134, composed a series of psalms, each of which is entitled 'A Song of Ascents'. These psalms were thought to be sung by Jews making a pilgrimage to Jerusalem as they ascended the steep hill to the city.

There is a type of the song of the Lord which, when sung either corporately or individually, creates a kind of spiritual elevator or lift. It operates especially through the vehicle of praise, though it can include any form of the song of the Lord which is sung in an inspiring and uplifting manner. For example, on one occasion when I was ministering at a conference in Canada, I experienced this uplifting manifestation in the prophetic songs of the Lord. One after another songs were put in my mouth, each with a greater degree of anointing than the previous one. This continued for over fifteen minutes. The power of God was so tangibly present that the holiness of the Lord manifested like fire in the room. It was almost like what is spoken of in Exodus 19:4—'You have seen what I did to the Egyptians, and how I bore you on eagles' wings, and brought you to Myself.' What a wonderful time we had in his presence.

Songs of ascents therefore are not confined to the expression of praise alone. But when the anointing of God is on songs of praise sung in an uplifting way, the hearts of the saints are lifted up before God. God's Spirit may be present in such a powerful way that the congregation can no longer stand on their feet, and may even be drawn to kneel. The higher you want to walk in the things of the Spirit, the lower you must bow in reverence.

Songs of ascents affect not only the spirit of man, but intensely motivate the mind, will and emotions as the whole being of each believer is caught up into the movement of the Spirit of God. One could say then that songs of ascents affect the very atmosphere of the building.

One evening, before I was scheduled to speak in a church meeting, we experienced this phenomenon of praise. Faith was so thick in the room that no one dared to move. Every believer seemed transfixed, caught into the waves of the Holy Spirit as he manifested his holy presence in our midst. I had already noted that the praise leaders had come in especially prepared and anointed. They communicated faith and celebration throughout the entire praise service; one song led into another, each more powerfully anointed than the last, until we arrived at a peak of praise, and God's glory fell. Then the people experienced a holy silence that no one broke for fear of grieving the Spirit of the Lord. The people stood, kneeled and lay prostrate before the Lord for fifteen to twenty minutes in awe of his presence. The songs of ascents created a spiritual doorway through which the Lord was able to minister to his people.

This occurrence is seldom seen in the expression of quiet worship. It will always begin with intense and fervent praise. Worship may then result owing to the uplifting of the Spirit, but only because of the awesome sense of God's glory filling the house.

Songs of witness

Moses and Joshua, walking side by side, drew near to the door of the Tent, bidden by the Lord. The inevitable was at hand. It was time for Moses to lay aside his physical temple and join the Lord in eternity. The time had come when Joshua would take his place and lead the people. As they came to the entrance of the sanctuary, the Lord's glory filled the Tent and he appeared to them in the pillar of cloud. There in that hallowed place, the holy and yet now-familiar voice began to speak of Moses' imminent death and future events concerning the people whom Moses had so faithfully led. There also in those final moments God mercifully gave to Moses the words of a song which in years to come would testify against Israel as a witness when they fell into sin and idolatry. (See Deuteronomy 31:14–22.)

Deuteronomy 31 and 32 are the only places in which such a song is mentioned in the Bible. God gave Moses the song of witness because he knew the heart of the people and that once they had entered the promised land and experienced satisfaction and blessing, they would deny him as their God and become worshippers of idols. They would break his covenant with them and eventually receive the due penalty for their actions. This song of witness would then be a constant reminder to them of his faithfulness, his commands and his covenant with them. Every person was to be taught the song; no one would be able to excuse their sinful actions. This song of witness would testify against them and prick their conscience in their time of rebellion.

Yet even with the song in their mouths and its truths set out clearly before them, the Hebrew children still fell away, forgetting the prophetic words and message. Innumerable songs of witness have been sung since that first one. The people of God have learned the truth and have still been disobedient. We have no excuse. I think it is time for us to believe him and pay heed to his songs, don't you?

6

The Song with a Double Anointing

> And from thence they went to Beer: that is the well whereof
> the Lord spake unto Moses, Gather the people together, and
> I will give them water. Then Israel sang this song, Spring up,
> O well; sing ye unto it: The princes digged the well, the
> nobles of the people digged it, by the direction of the law-
> giver, with their staves (Num 21:16–18, KJV).

The people were thirsty. They had arrived at Beer to find
that the well was stopped up. Such a situation was potentially explosive as Moses knew from past experience: a
thirsty people can be a desperate people. At the Lord's
command, Moses gathered the people together to await
the Lord's provision of water; the well at Beer would have
to be dug anew.

Thousands of Christians today are facing the same predicament of heart. They thirst for the springs of living
water and yet they have neglected the very fountain of life
within them. They are spiritually stopped up. Yet the
potential for the waters to be restored is there. How can
these wells be unlocked again? Every promise the Lord
gives requires personal, responsible co-operation and
obedience. He makes the promises! We must then walk
out his word through to completion in patience. In these

verses from Numbers 21 we find a spiritual model that is like a key able to unlock the doors of the fountains of the Spirit inside every believer. How did they use this key?

Unstopping the wells of living water within

First of all, the people gathered together under Moses' leadership. God promised to give them water once they were gathered. Then something strange but of spiritual significance happened. Israel sang to the well! It was a custom in ancient Eastern cultures that when a well was to be dug, the people would stand around it in a group and sing to it a song designed to release the waters. This custom represents a spiritual principle. Wells, according to the Scriptures, are symbolic of churches, ministries and the well-spring of life within the individual. Natural wells may need to be tapped. When they become blocked up with the filth of sin and the refuse of carnality so also the spiritual wells of churches, ministries, etc., frequently need to be re-opened. Moses used a spiritual principle to unlock a natural well so that the people would not die of thirst.

Secondly, they sang to the well because the 'lawgiver' directed them to (v 18). This lawgiver was most probably Moses. Moses stood in the office of prophet and therefore his direction had prophetic implications. The term prophetic, frequently distorted, basically means having spiritual insight into the things of God. Moses functioned in this in a powerful sense because he was also a prophet by calling and ministry. He is the one who gave the direction to dig this well.

The word for 'song' in Numbers 21:17 belongs to the *shir* group; but the verb for 'sing' in 'sing ye unto it' is of a different type and tells us something about *how* the song was sung.

The *anah* song of the Lord in unlocking the spiritual wells

The way in which they sang to the well is indicated by the Hebrew verb *anah*, which means 'to answer in singing'. The type of corporate singing that was used in Numbers 21:17 was one that packs a double punch as the people repeat the leader's words. It is almost like a spiritual jack-hammer. The song repeatedly and powerfully pummels away all hindrances restricting the water's flow. Under prophetic supervision, it is a powerful tool for deliverance and release for the waters of the Spirit. The church need not thirst. The waters need to be loosed and such a song will loose them.

How the wells become blocked

Wells which are not regularly tended can easily become blocked. Sometimes this happens by accident. But sometimes it is the result of foul play, as it was in the case of Isaac's wells as related in Genesis 26. Despite the famine which prevailed in Gerar, Isaac's flocks were prospering; this aroused the envy of the inhabitants of Gerar, the Philistines, who were faring less well than Isaac. They therefore poured earth into Isaac's wells to prevent his flocks from drinking. There is a parallel in the modern church. Many churches and individual Christians have been attacked by the same vice as the Philistines. Jealousy has bred competition and hate which have blocked the wells of individual believers and churches. The song of the Lord can re-open these wells.

Have we been guilty of hewing out broken cisterns which hold no spiritual water? Have we neglected the fountains of living waters? (See Jeremiah 2:13.) The Lord is our fountain of living waters. As we sing unto him we unleash the power of his Spirit. This demands a daily relationship. We cannot live off the experience of yesterday's relationship. We must dig the wells once again in the church—individually, corporately and ministerially—before it's too late and perishing believers die of thirst unnecessarily.

Anah in the song of the Lord in praise

We have seen how the people sang (*anah*) to the well; this type of singing is also used in offering praise and thanks to the Lord. There are only a few references to this in Scripture and we will look at them briefly.

One example is in Psalm 147:7: 'Sing to the Lord with thanksgiving.' Thanksgiving was frequently accompanied by lifting the arms in a sacrifice of praise and thanks, which indicates that a yielded heart is important in singing this song.

This type of song was also ministered when the foundation of the Temple was laid, in Ezra 3:10–11. As the people sang, they mixed their singing with loud shouts and radical expressions of praise. This song can be explosive when it is done at the correct time and is inspired from the heart.

The Hebrew children also sang praise in this way after God delivered them from the Egyptians at the Red Sea (Exod 15). Their song was born out of rejoicing. Moses and the people sang of the mighty acts of God and Miriam answered them (*anah*), repeating their account of his triumph (v 21). These truths, declared twice, had a double anointing. In Hosea 2:14–15, God promised that he would once more grant his people to sing (*anah*) as they did in the days of their youth, when they came out of Egypt. This promise of the doubly anointed, joyful song will be restored to the people of God who have been in a spiritual wilderness. It will be heard again before Jesus returns.

7

Songs of Joyful Faith and Triumph

Sing, O daughter of Zion! Shout, O Israel! Be glad and rejoice with all your heart, O daughter of Jerusalem! The Lord has taken away your judgments, He has cast out your enemy. The King of Israel, the Lord, is in your midst; you shall see disaster no more. In that day it shall be said to Jerusalem: 'Do not fear; Zion, let not your hands be weak. The Lord your God in your midst, the Mighty One, will save; He will rejoice over you with gladness, He will quiet you with His love, He will rejoice over you with singing' (Zeph 3:14–17).

Zephaniah 3 is rich with understanding concerning the Lord's song. In a previous chapter we saw how we are called to imitate the song which God sings. This demands of us the utmost humility, an absolute freedom from the fear of man and the joyful unashamed expression that only his presence can inspire.

The daughter of Zion was *commanded* to sing such a song. As we have seen, *ranan*, the Hebrew verb translated as 'sing' in verse 1, is used of a song that sounds like a loud, joyful cry of triumph. The primary purpose of this type of song is praise. This song of praise is built on intense emotion. Without that depth of feeling it is half-hearted, a cheap imitation.

This type of the song of the Lord is one which challenges more Christians than any other. It's amazing to me that people who are unafraid to shout and joyfully praise their favourite sports team are frequently too embarrassed to give loud praise to the King of kings. I've heard countless excuses for this timid behaviour. But none of those excuses is justified when compared to God's word. Are our attitudes based upon God's word or do we esteem our culture, our personality traits and family backgrounds more highly than the Scriptures? Considering this, I find myself becoming irate at the way we ignore biblical truths. How can we continue to defend our reserved behaviour when we give the world more than we give God? Our greatest hindrance in the song of the Lord is self-absorption. Could we be so concerned about what everyone else thinks about us that we virtually deny the truth of God's word in order to satisfy our flesh? Let us obey God's commands.

Songs of joyful praise marking a change of spiritual season

It is obvious by now that praise is one of the most common types of the song of the Lord; yet there are certain spiritual seasons when it has special significance. Ecclesiastes 3:1 states that 'to everything there is a time and a season'. There are also certain times and seasons when this form of the song of the Lord in praise is at its highest level of intensity: though it should always be functioning in the praise life of the church and individual, it is most vibrant at those times which mark a new move or fresh blessing of God. Psalm 30:5 says 'For His anger is but for a moment, His favor is for life; weeping may endure for a night, but joy comes in the morning.' The word 'joy' here is *rinnah*, the noun derived from *ranan*. Sometimes the night seasons can feel dreadfully long, especially when a struggle is raging in your heart. During such times, have you ever found yourself looking anxiously for the morning to arrive? The morning represents hope for a new beginning.

When the Hebrew children left Egypt, they sang a song of intense joy. When Deborah saw the defeat of Sisera, she too sang an ardent, poetic tribute of joy. When David and all Israel transported the Ark of the Covenant to Jerusalem, theirs was also an extremely powerful song. The list could go on and on. We must recognise from the pattern revealed in these examples that whenever the sun is setting on an old move of God and a new era is about to dawn this type of praise breaks forth. Psalm 65:8 states that God makes the outgoings of morning and evening to rejoice: 'They also who dwell in the farthest parts are afraid of Your signs; You make the outgoings of the morning and evening *rejoice*.' The Hebrew verb used for rejoice here is *ranan*. These songs, then, are most powerful in the early stages of a new move of the Spirit of God, such as times of revival within the church or the times of harvest which follow.

What is it that causes this song to be born in the seasons of the spiritual morning? First of all, morning is the time when God's mercy is fresh and new. Secondly, morning is a time when God sends the manna. Spiritual food inspires great joy, even more than natural food. Let us now look at the songs of revival and the songs of harvest.

Songs of revival challenge the church

Times of change in the cycle of spiritual seasons are marked by exuberant, powerful praise. But what happens in the middle of the cycle? Sadly, the original vibrancy of the songs is gradually lost; as time passes, the people of God are weakened by doubt and become increasingly introspective and legalistic. As each season draws to an end, their relationship with God becomes shallow and dominated by intellect; the traditions of man become more precious than the first love of the Lord. In such a condition the church will prefer to sing songs which are quiet and restrained. Thus when the time of transition is at hand, the loud, joyful songs which herald the new season of revival in the church are unwelcome and controversy arises as these songs force believers to confront the passivity and carnality of their lifestyle. This spirit of controversy is the sin of which Michal, David's wife, was guilty. She despised this type of joyful song and as a result she was cursed and bore no children. (See 2 Samuel 6:14–22.)

Every time the church despises this type of the song of the Lord, it is in danger of becoming like Michal: childless and refused of God. This type of song is one of the spiritual alarms indicating that the fresh winds of revival—and the times of harvest which follow—have begun. It is extremely hazardous for the believer who does not take heed of these alarms. We could miss out in the Last Days if we don't learn to recognise the signs of the changing seasons of God. Change is in the wind! Will you recognise it and respond to this type of the song of the Lord as it arises, or will you despise the song and be a fruitless tree? The choice is entirely up to you.

There is hope, however, for the churches that have become childless but truly repent of their sin:

'Sing, O barren, you who have not borne! Break forth into singing, and cry aloud, you who have not labored with child! For more are the children of the desolate than the children of the married woman,' says the Lord. 'Enlarge the place of your tent, and let them stretch out the curtains of your dwellings; do not spare; lengthen your cords, and strengthen your stakes. For you shall expand to the right and to the left, and your descendants will inherit the nations, and make the desolate cities inhabited' (Is 54:1–3).

For those who turn to the Lord and repent of their rebellious ways, *growth is inevitable*.

In Isaiah 54, God commands the one who is barren to sing. She who was childless and refused by God was to cease her mourning and break forth into a loud and joyful noise with the *ranan* radical song of praise. Why would she have to 'break forth'? Bound by the chains of shame and silent mourning, her voice had been restrained through grief and the feelings of being forsaken. Shame is only driven away when room is made for God's glory and honour to manifest.

This condition of heart is becoming prevalent today. Fruitless and feeling forgotten, Christians are slowly coming to their senses and recognising the need to repent of their hardness of heart and unfaithfulness. It is possible that their barrenness was caused by their rejection of the songs of revival in previous moves of the Spirit; but by the grace of God this same song will also deliver them.

God is calling his people to a restored relationship. The door which they once refused to enter is open to those who will yield their heart to him unashamedly and break forth into joyful, loving abandon and song.

The results of such restoration are remarkable. Childlessness is replaced by fruitfulness. The grave-clothes are replaced with garments of praise. Grief is replaced with growth on every side. Mercy is given instead of shame and reproach. What wonderful possibilities await those who will sing his song of joy!

It is time to break forth in the song of joyful praise. As we enter into the season of his return, let us learn to be satisfied with his mercy early in the season of his timing. If we are satisfied we will rejoice for the rest of our days: 'Oh, satisfy us early with Your mercy, that we may rejoice [*ranan*] and be glad all our days!' (Ps 90:14).

Before moving on from songs of revival to songs of harvest, let us consider a song which is relevant to both:

Songs of fervent prayer

Once, when I was speaking in Sweden on the subject of prayer, I shared some teaching about the validity and power of the scriptural practice of sung prayer. As I was speaking, I noticed that my interpreter was having a rather difficult time speaking. Then, right in the middle of the message, she began to weep. She continued to interpret, until finally she paused. With tears in her eyes, she began to explain to me that for the past several months she had been prompted to sing out her prayer to the Lord. Sometimes this prayer song would be so intense that she would want to cry out. The reason she was so moved while interpreting for me was because she suddenly realised that God had been moving in her all those months. She had been so afraid that it wasn't scriptural that she had tried to restrain this song of the Lord. Overjoyed by the truth she had heard, she would restrain the song no longer.

In some places in Scripture, prayer is referred to as a *cry*, using the Hebrew word *rinnah* (the noun from *ranan*). Let us look at this song of the Lord and see how it works in prayer.

This type of song appears to have been ministered by individuals, such as Solomon and David. All songs in the *ranan/rinnah* category are born out of the deepest emotion; they are fervent and full of confident faith and love. When they are in the form of prayer, they are supremely prayers of faith, however desperate the circumstances may be.

Solomon sang this type of prayer at the dedication of the Temple; it was a joyful cry of faith and triumph (2 Chron 6:19). David cried out in this song of prayer when he was in trouble, and was confident that God would hear him (Ps 61). Psalm 17 is another such prayer; let us notice that in verse 1 David states that his prayer was 'not from deceitful lips'. His words and his motives were sincere. How frequently Christians try to 'con' God, using manipulative words and deceitful phrases! But God is Spirit and they who seek him must do so in spirit and in truth.

This song of the Lord in prayer is one of the most sincere expressions of faith available to the believer.

This type of song believes that God will deliver his people; no matter how difficult the circumstances, he will be faithful. John Wesley once said that it seemed God wouldn't move in the earth until someone prayed. As the early morning dawns for revival and harvest in the earth, could it be that God is waiting for the church to arise and sing this prayer and cry of faith? It is time to arise and sing!

The joyful triumphant song of harvest

The song of harvest is different from the song of revival. As we have seen, songs of revival initiate the renewal of a backslidden church and the restoration of its relationship with God. Once this has been achieved there will follow a harvest in all areas of God's good and perfect will for his church and then the songs of harvest will be heard.

Before looking in detail at these songs, let us first consider the nature of the harvest, how it is produced and its relation to revival. In the time leading up to revival and restoration God's people will have shed many tears. For some, these will have been tears of repentance as they were finally brought to recognise their lack of love for God. Others, long aware of the barrenness of their lives, will have wept at their unfruitfulness. Some will have wept and prayed over unfulfilled hopes and dreams. We may be tempted to think that these tears have no positive value. But Psalm 126:5–6 suggests something quite different. 'Those who sow in tears shall reap in joy' (v 5). Those who weep as they make heartfelt intercession, or in true repentance, or with a deep sense of need are in fact sowing the seeds of joy. Such tears are power-packed seeds which in due time produce a varied harvest.

Revival itself is produced by these 'tear seeds', and a backslidden church is restored to relationship with God. There is also then a rich harvest of lives made fruitful, and hopes and dreams are fulfilled; and the patient faith and endurance of many are rewarded. God's people will reap this harvest with joy and sing the triumphant song of harvest. When we see a manifestation of the dynamic praise which characterises the beginning of revival we can expect the song of harvest to follow.

Reaping is a time of great rejoicing which issues in shouting, singing, dancing and total abandonment to loving Jesus. It's as if God's people have been released from bondage. The verses from Psalm 126 which we noted above speak about the tears which the Jews wept during their captivity in Babylon. Their tears were turned to joy when they were released and their mouths were filled with laughter and singing (v 2).

But the song of harvest is not only an expression of joy at the harvest which is being gathered. It also produces a further harvest. The Christian who sings this song does not return empty-handed. This song of the Lord is like a sickle to bring in the sheaves: when the world hears this song, hearts are convicted and souls are saved. People have never heard a song like it before and most of them don't know that Christianity has something so wonderful to offer them. The salvation of souls is yet further cause for rejoicing.

Because it is not complicated, this song will unfortunately be challenged by the complex, intellectual Christian. This song is a simple cry of faith, not the product of sophisticated mental processes. Those who have a shallow relationship with God will view this song as mere emotion. But this must not deter us from singing it. In addition to expressing the joy of harvest and touching the hearts of unbelievers, this song has another vital function at harvest time: it releases the strength which the labourer needs to bring in the sheaves.

Just as human adrenaline causes the body to perform unusual feats of strength in times of danger and stress, so the song of harvest is like a spiritual adrenaline that enables the Christian labourer to accomplish the work that harvest requires. Harvest is the most costly and demanding season the farmer faces. Innumerable Christians have wept countless tears in prayer. Their strength is spent. As the time of harvest draws nigh this song of the Lord imparts the necessary strength to weary souls—and it will last throughout the harvest produced by these tear seeds. The song of harvest is about to be heard in the earth. Prepare your heart, church! Prepare your heart, believer! He will bring forth his people with joyful singing so that they can reap.

The body of Christ must be awakened to recognise how it has been seduced by the powers of darkness and allowed the idolatrous Babylonian lifestyle to captivate it. It must answer the call that the Lord has given and come out before it's too late. The song of harvest was given to the Judaean captives only after they had left Babylon. Whatever idols have been embraced must be cast to the ground. God will only give this song of harvest to a people sold out to him and him alone.

The song of the redeemed

God has built and is building a supernatural highway for the Last Days. It is a highway of holiness; a highway upon which the unclean cannot pass.

Isaiah 35:8–10 speaks prophetically of an exodus involving both Jews and backslidden Christians. In the last few years, thousands and thousands of Jews have left their homes and moved to Israel. Yet this immense company is only a portion of those who will eventually walk on this holy highway. There is also an innumerable throng of backsliders who also need to return to the Lord in a spiritual sense. They too must walk on that highway.

These two groups, however different, can be identified as the ransomed of the Lord, who will return to Zion and the Lord. The ransomed of the Lord will sing (*ranan*) one of the most joyful songs of praise and gladness mentioned in the Old Testament (Is 35:10). Before this song is born, the hearts and lives of those called to walk this holy path will suffer oppression from the enemy, other people and adverse circumstances. They will sorrow and mourn; but this oppression will ultimately be the cause of their resolve to return to the Lord.

We haven't as yet heard such a song. It could be compared to the joyful song that the Hebrew children sang as they left Egypt's cruel bondage. The song was born out of sheer thanksgiving and relief. This song of the redeemed will drive sorrow and vexation away. The deep, heartfelt agony and sighing will flee from those who sing it, for God will give them a joy such as they have never known. When unbelievers also, unprompted by the saved, turn to the Lord and begin to sing such a song, it will be a sure sign that God is moving mightily.

This song is indeed prophetic and unique. Though it hasn't yet been sung be sure that it will soon be heard in the earth.

The joyful song of praise before the battle

The battle lines were drawn and a sense of foreboding loomed over the land like a dark and ominous thundercloud. An innumerable enemy host was advancing towards Judah; fear's cold fingers gripped the heart of Jehoshaphat, King of Judah, as he heard the report of them. Helplessness overwhelmed him. The odds were, naturally speaking, insurmountable. Judah, the God-given inheritance of the people of Jehovah, would lose everything they had worked for, everything they'd invested their lives in, unless God himself intervened. Reaching into the depths of his heart, at a time when natural understanding fails, Jehoshaphat set himself to seek the Lord, and he called the people of Judah to assemble together to fast and ask the Lord for help. A reverent fear of God, mixed with a sense of vulnerability and dependence pervaded the assembly as Jehoshaphat lifted his voice to the Lord on behalf of Judah. In his prayer, Jehoshaphat recalled God's promises concerning Judah. It was clear that Judah would be powerless against their adversaries—surely defeated—unless God intervened. In pleading desperation, Jehoshaphat's final cry revealed the helplessness he felt, crying out, 'We don't know what to do!' But in nearly the same breath, faith resounded in his next words, 'But our eyes are upon you!' (See 2 Chronicles 20.)

Faced by seemingly impossible odds, Christians throughout the world have uttered similar cries. The words 'I don't know what to do' have verbalised the helplessness of countless numbers of people. The battle lines have been clearly drawn. But, in the face of such disadvantage, whose battle is it?

As Judah stood before God, awaiting an answer, so today's Christian stands as well. The answer then was simple and still applies today. The message was clear: the battle is not ours, but the Lord's. The Lord fought for Judah then, and the Lord will fight for those who will praise him now. He hasn't changed and awaits those who will let him take up their cause. But what does this trust require? What actions and steps of faith need to emerge in order to bring forth a triumphant people?

God was not asking his people to be passive and inactive in this time of battle, and nor must they be so today. Judah saw the salvation of the Lord because they obeyed his command and believed his words. God didn't need their help. He wanted their co-operation.

His command to them was to hearken to his words. This they did. Secondly, he told them not to be afraid of the multitude of the enemy host, reminding them that it was his battle, not theirs. This they did. Thirdly, he instructed them to go down against their enemy. This they did. They didn't run from their enemy—they faced them on their own territory. Fourthly, he reminded them that they would not need to fight in this battle, but they were to set themselves in a position of readiness and stand still to see the salvation of God. God had spoken and answered their cry. Gratefully, Jehoshaphat and all the people of Judah prostrated themselves before the Lord in thankful worship.

Arising early the following morning, Jehoshaphat encouraged the people, reminding them that if they would believe God and believe his prophets, then he would establish them and they would prosper.

Finally, the moment of truth arrived. After consulting with the people, Jehoshaphat appointed singers, skilled and approved in their ministry. These singers went out, positioned in front of the army, with their arms extended towards the heavens saying, 'Praise the Lord, for his mercy endures for ever!' What a strange sight they must have been! Then as they marched in front of the army, they began to sing. The Hebrew word for 'sing' in verse 22 is of the *ranan* type: their singing was loud, triumphant and faith-filled. Mixed with the sincere praises of their hearts, it created a spiritual door through which God could work and move. While they sang in such a demonstrative manner God set up a spiritual ambush and the enemy began to turn upon themselves. They fought each other until they were utterly destroyed. As Jehoshaphat and the people closed in upon the massacre, the spoils of war gleamed in the daylight, waiting to be gathered. It took three days for the victorious Jews to collect all the spoil, there was so much. Jewels, gold, garments—there was an abundance of natural wealth to be gathered. But what if they hadn't been obedient? What if they had cried out in unbelief instead of faith-filled praise? The answer is plain. There would have been no victory. Jerusalem would have been destroyed and ransacked. They would have faced utter destruction, losing not only their natural investments, but also the spiritual inheritance promised them by God. All of this great victory was due to the fact that they obeyed the Lord. He heard their cry and he answered with victory.

Still, how does this apply to the Christian today?

Churches, ministers and lay persons are facing some of the most incredible times ever to exist on this earth. Tremendous challenge lies ahead for all in the days to come. How will believers deal with such trauma? In the natural realm, the odds don't look great. Like Jehoshaphat, Christians are beginning to cry out, 'We don't know what to do!' Will we turn our eyes to the Lord or will we become fearful and eventually defeated? These are our options. But we are not left without help and tools.

The powerful song of joyful praise will probably be one of the most valuable tools for deliverance in the Last Days. It will be especially so concerning financial struggles and business. The praising Christian will be the triumphant Christian. Those who willingly yield their voices to that loud, triumphant song will not only see spiritual victory, but natural blessing as well. The individual who believes God and his prophets will be established and prosper. What a powerful truth, with a fantastic promise. How sad that some will not heed this word of hope.

When offered in the face of extreme struggle, this song must be ministered to the Lord from a sincere and trusting heart; it cannot be used in a manipulative fashion. God knows the heart, honouring that which is born of unfeigned faith. I don't think there is any other type of song in the Scriptures which demonstrates such absolute radical style; it requires greater fearlessness and emotional abandon than any other. When it is sung in times of battle, God hears and answers, giving us far above what we can ask or think. This song is similar to the song of harvest, because it endues ability for reaping. But it is reserved for the battlefield. When you don't know what to do, turn your eyes upon him and sing! He will fight the battle for you!

8

Songs of Deliverance

It was a hot and humid summer afternoon. I had felt the presence of the Lord in such a sweet way all that day and sensed a witness in my spirit that something unusual was going to happen. Picking up my guitar, I found a cool spot to sit and began to sing to the Lord quiet and gentle songs of praise and worship. It seemed as if a refreshing stream bubbled forth as I sang new songs never sung before. At some point in the worship the song changed, and the bubbling stream increased its intensity, becoming a rushing river. Prophetically inspired words spontaneously began to pour out through my lips. This was a song of the Lord for me—possibly for someone else at a later time. I grabbed a piece of paper and a pen and began to scribble down the words as quickly as they came. 'You were found in the high places where the battles have been waged. You've been seasoned by your servanthood; in wisdom you have aged . . .' It went on and on, until 'Eagle Song', a song of deliverance, was born. My heart was encouraged and touched. When, years later, I recorded the song, I had no idea what Jesus would do with it to minister to someone's needy life.

She was lying in a hospital room, totally paralysed; a prisoner in her own body. She was a victim of Hodgkin's disease and a very, very ill woman. Before this attack she had pioneered and pastored a successful and growing church in a small country town in the state of Nebraska. Now she could do nothing but lie there. The doctors had tried everything, including wrong things. An incorrect drug prescription had placed her in this frozen state. Her auditory senses were so magnified that she couldn't tolerate any sound. A student of the Scriptures, she couldn't endure even the familiar sound of the Bible as it was read and played over a cassette recorder. She felt helpless, she felt alone. But her strong faith in God would not let her give up.

Then she discovered one exception to her inability to tolerate sound; she had acquired one of my recordings of 'Eagle Song' and, despite her desperate condition, was able to listen to it. She took its prophetic message to heart. She would win this battle—she and the Lord. He would set her free from this work of Satan. She would fly again. She listened to the tape over and over again. The incorrect drug prescription was discovered and corrected, and her paralysis disappeared. Gradually and miraculously she regained the lost ground and today she is completely healed, back in the ministry and pastoring her flock with tremendous wisdom and love.

Since she shared her testimony with me, I have often wondered what would have happened if I hadn't listened to the Lord that summer afternoon many years ago. God would have no doubt found another tool, but it was such a joy to my heart to be a small part of the miracle and to see him work in her life, setting her free from such a terrible illness, so that she could serve him again.

In Psalm 32:7, as we've seen before, David talks about the songs and shouts of deliverance which he had heard in the hiding place of the presence of God: 'You are my hiding place; You shall preserve me from trouble; You shall surround me with songs of deliverance.' These songs of deliverance are most frequently ministered in the times of personal prayer, praise and worship. There comes a time, though, when they are to be ministered to those unable to enter into the reality of his presence for themselves. Proverbs 12:6 states that the mouth of the upright brings deliverance: 'The words of the wicked are, "Lie in wait for blood," but the mouth of the upright will deliver them.' As God's Spirit anoints, we are called to proclaim liberty to those who are captives. Jesus came to set the captives free. We are his ambassadors, his representatives on the earth. If we abide in the shadow of his wing, hearing his delivering melodies, we too can become instruments of expression for his songs of deliverance.

Ministering the song of deliverance to the oppressed

King Saul was depressed. Though once anointed of God, he had rebelliously turned against the Lord and lost that precious anointing. Now plagued by an evil spirit, he could find no relief from his torment. Only when David, who was a gifted minstrel, came and ministered to Saul, did the troubled man find relief. David ministered songs of deliverance to King Saul and brought God's delivering anointing. (See 1 Samuel 16:14–23.) This ministry was successful, however, only while David was able to retain favour in Saul's sight. Later, jealousy of David began to stir in the heart of King Saul as David grew in reputation and honour among the people. Another fit of depression settled on the king and once again David returned to play the songs of deliverance. But Saul's attitude to David had changed and the songs of deliverance were limited in their effect. (See 1 Samuel 18:10–12.) Deliverance through such songs is only granted to those who desire freedom. Saul only wished David's death. Deliverance would not come, and Saul's torment continued.

The ministry of the songs of deliverance to captives, tormented souls and afflicted bodies is only successful if ministered to those who truly desire liberty. The purpose of these songs of deliverance is to help those who can no longer help themselves; God's mercy and compassion are extended through these melodies. His love will never break the human will. Liberty comes to those who seek him and trust his faithful hand to set them free.

When Jesus walked on the earth, for most of the time he only ministered to those who sought him out, in faith, for their freedom. Should we be any different? The ministry of the song of the Lord cannot be forced upon anyone. Sadly, some people really don't want to be free. They enjoy, and are comfortable in, their captivity. With a discerning eye, let us look for those who possess faith and who truly desire to receive deliverance. However, this does not mean that we should neglect opportunities for revealing his great love to those who appear uninterested. We must provide them with an opportunity to choose life, yet without forcing their will. The believer who ministers the song of the Lord has to have a discerning heart, without a critical spirit. Whenever we can attain that difficult balance of compassion and wisdom, the song of the Lord will be most effective. Perhaps someone is waiting for you to receive a song of deliverance which will help them in their time of need. Listen, then, as you hide in the shadow of his wing and one day he will possibly give such a song to you. Then, at the proper time, you will be used to set the captives free.

9

The Song that Leaves an Indelible Mark

Every once in a while, God plants the seeds for a specifically rare and unusual song of the Lord. This song tends to etch such an impression upon the listener's heart that those who hear it are never the same again. The chisel of this song of the Lord engraves an indelible mark upon the soul.

Each word, note and anointing of these songs becomes the engraving tool in the Master Sculptor's strong hands. With tremendous precision, the Spirit of God knows exactly when such a song is to be born and then ministered. These songs are often popular and should not be tampered with in any way. It is impossible to alter them without damaging them.

Music composers of nearly every generation have dreamed of writing a song which will survive the passage of time and remain as a statement on the earth. Few such songs have ever been born.

A famous example of this type of song is Handel's *Messiah*, which, hundreds of years after its miraculous birth, can still be heard throughout the entire world. Handel was a man who had been granted the privilege of hearing one of the finest works of music ever to be sung for the glory of God. He was also a man who had learned to listen to the Lord's song, as ministered to him by the Spirit, and then communicate it to others—a small sample of heaven's song on earth. To tamper with it would be a tragedy. Not all of us are Handels, though.

Different degrees of anointing

This type of song has different degrees of anointing. It may be born simply for the purpose of ministering to a needy individual's heart, in which case, once it is sung to them it may never be sung again. Yet when it was heard, it engraved an indelible mark upon the heart of the listener, and his or her needs were met.

Ministering the song to an individual

After I had finished speaking at a church in Jefferson, Iowa, one particular evening, I felt directed by the Spirit of God to invite those who desired to receive ministry to kneel at the front of the sanctuary for prayer. As was my custom at the time, I proceeded to the piano and began to lead the congregation in a few worship choruses before praying for the personal needs of those kneeling. During that time of worship, the Spirit of God manifested himself in the sanctuary with tremendous might. Many in the congregation wept as they knelt near their pew or at the altar.

Caught up in the presence of the Lord, a young woman in her early twenties sat in the front pew. While singing, I had a strong witness in my heart that a prophetic song was about to be born for her. As I opened my mouth in faith, the words of the prophetic song rolled out in melodic grace. Cautiously, so as not to instil false hope or direction, I sang without indicating that the song was for her. When a song is born of God's will and Spirit, it will witness to the individual's heart and produce a commitment and a response from them. This type of song should never be forced upon believers. They must know for themselves that God has spoken. Listening intently to the message, holding her head in her hands, she began to weep. God was speaking to her, tenderly communicating to her about a decision she was contemplating. Quietly, she slipped up to the altar and knelt. Committing her life to the Lord, her future was placed into his guiding hands. This song engraved a mark upon her heart that permanently influenced her future and led her into the will of the Lord for her life.

Songs which leave an indelible mark on a group

My husband and I were part of a prayer tour to Israel led by Steven Lightle. I was responsible for leading much of the praise and worship and ministering prophetic song as the Spirit of the Lord led. On that tour, God gave me a song which made an indelible mark on the entire prayer tour group and leaders.

Approximately twenty-four hours before ministering the song I was conscious of an inward witness in my heart that God had planted the seeds for something incredibly special in my spirit. No words had yet been given, but the anointing of God began to increase in its intensity like a fermenting wine, until I knew it was almost time for the message to explode. Our tour group was scheduled to cross the Sea of Galilee to Capernaum in a small tourist boat. We would take communion while out on the waters before arriving at Capernaum for a time of teaching and prayer. After boarding the boat, I mentioned to Steven and Judy Lightle that I believed a song was going to be born. Steven felt we needed to wait until we arrived at Capernaum and had heard the preaching of the word. I would then minister the still unknown message and song. Communication among leaders is absolutely necessary in order for a prophetic song to be most effective and anointed.

The little outdoor chapel near Capernaum was constructed of wooden poles and palm branches, and was situated on the shore of the Sea of Galilee. As the waves glided in, you could hear them gently lapping up against the rocks. There in that tranquil little sanctuary the song would be born. Steven preached a powerful and convicting message entitled 'King of the Breadmakers'. Like freshly ploughed soil, the hearts of the people were finally ready to receive the song after the delivery of Steven's anointed word. With the guitar slung over my shoulder, I began in simple, hopeful trust to pluck the strings, seeking to be sensitive to the anointing of the Spirit. Like a sweeping flood bursting through a bank the spontaneous words began to rush out. Each utterance was punctuated by the power of the Spirit, penetrating passive hearts. A holy hush blanketed the tour group for the entire duration of the song, as the people were called to repentance and faith. Then, mingled with the sound of the waves I heard the deep sobbing cries of some of the group; others remained silent in earnest reflection. God was at work. His spiritual chisel had engraved a message of commitment and faith into the hearts of every person present. No one dared to speak, his presence was so very evident.

A song born in times of trouble

Songs of this type are born out of times of adversity and brokenness. They are fashioned from the fires of faith in the midst of trial and persecution. Perhaps this will be a notable factor to consider in the Last Days. If the body of Christ is bound to face persecution, such tribulation may create an atmosphere conducive to the creation of songs which leave an indelible mark. God will challenge and encourage his people through these songs. Prepare your ears to listen: the chisel is in the Master's hand!

10

Massa—the Burden of the Song of the Lord

The oxen had stopped. Off to the side of the wooden cart the limp body of Uzza lay quiet. He was dead. Moments before, Chenaniah had seen Uzza sitting alongside his brother Ahio, dutifully guiding the new cart towards Jerusalem. Suddenly, as the procession of jubilant marchers approached the rugged ground near the threshing floor of Chidon, the oxen had faltered on the rocky pathway, shaking the wagon and its contents. Unaware of the impending judgement, Uzza had leaned backwards, stretching his arm towards the Ark of the Covenant, attempting to steady it. Before anyone knew what had happened Uzza was dead, stricken and judged by God. Screaming in terror, Ahio and those nearest the vehicle watched as Uzza fell limply from the wagon onto the ground. Fear spread through the parade like the piercing cold wind on a winter night. Instead of joyful shouts of praise, mournful cries arose as word circulated through the crowd. Holy fear permeated the atmosphere. Stooping over Uzza's dead body, David King of Israel cried out in furious agony.

Observing from the sidelines, Chenaniah, chief of the Levites, realised the gravity of the situation. This matter of moving the Ark of the Covenant to Jerusalem was a lot more than just an issue of simple transportation. This was no ordinary piece of furniture. It had been many years since Israel had recognised the need for the Ark. But David, yearning to restore it to its rightful place, had sought to bring it to Jerusalem. Chenaniah reasoned that God must have a better method of doing it.

Three months passed. Wondering how to bring the Ark to Jerusalem, David grieved. He now understood that preparation was of the utmost importance and pitched a tent, ready for the Ark to rest in. Then, having sought the prescribed order of the Lord in the Scriptures, he determined that the Levites were to carry the Ark upon their shoulders as commanded by God; it should never have been transported in a wooden cart. The Levites and priests obediently accepted the tasks to which they were assigned. Uzza's death still remained fresh in their memories. This time they would do it God's way.

Conscious of a tremendous weight of responsibility, Chenaniah pondered his assignment. He had been appointed to lead the thousands of singers in their singing. Hundreds of instruments—trumpets, cymbals, psalteries and harps—would be sounded in the massive procession. Somehow he would have to organise that sound into a unified, holy presentation. He would need strength and sensitivity to co-ordinate the movements of the Ark as it was carried step by ordered step towards Jerusalem. There would be sacrifices of seven rams and seven bulls and the singing would need to harmonise with the sacrificial actions. Indeed, his responsibility was very great. He would literally bear the *burden* of the song of the Lord.

A vivid picture is painted in 1 Chronicles 13 and 15. The death of Uzza should impress upon our hearts the seriousness of this matter. Lack of preparation resulted in that man's needless death. In painful reflection, David prepared a proper plan. This format included a more excellent organisation of the music. Chenaniah was selected for that leadership and was well able to accomplish the task: 'Chenaniah, leader of the Levites, was instructor in charge of the music, because he was skillful . . .' (1 Chron 15:22).

Bearing the burden of the song of the Lord as Chenaniah did

In 1 Chronicles 15:27, Chenaniah is identified as the 'master of the song'. An unusual Hebrew word is used here for 'song': the word is *massa*, which is defined as 'a burden, something to be carried, a prophecy, a song or a tribute'. *Massa* is most commonly defined as 'burden' which in almost every instance, refers to a prophetic burden or vision from the Lord. This song of the Lord is essentially a song of great weightiness, prophetic in nature and with the purpose of lifting up tribute to God. Some translations of this word imply that Chenaniah bore the burden of the song. Throughout the years in which I've led praise and worship, I have found that leading the corporate song can be a great burden indeed, especially if I become aware that the congregation is unresponsive.

This concept of the song of the Lord being a burden is very important, especially when considering corporate praise and worship. It is also significant that this song burden occurred at a season of change. God's presence was moving and his people co-operated as they moved with the presence. The burden of the song of the Lord, as illustrated in these chapters, is at its height in such a season. Chenaniah bore that burden. The huge responsibility of leading and exercising authority so that there would be an anointing on the song rested upon his shoulders. Some valuable lessons can be learned by examining the brief ministry of this man.

Mentioned only three times in the Scriptures, Chenaniah's name means 'that which is planted or established by Jehovah'. Like a mighty oak tree, he glorified God, allowing God to establish his ministry. He possessed the necessary qualifications to minister in the role of master of the song.

According to 1 Chronicles 15:22, Chenaniah was *skilful*. The Hebrew word is *mebin*, which means 'intelligent, wise, discerning'. Natural talent and ability were not the only qualities Chenaniah possessed. Using spiritual insight and wisdom and his knowledge of the ministry of the song of the Lord he was able to distinguish between good and evil. He was able to recognise potential problems and solve them quickly.

Bearing the responsibility and burden of the song, it was necessary for Chenaniah to be perceptive in discerning the needs of the various situations and to follow the leading of the Spirit of God. Despite this ability in the ministry of the song of the Lord, the Scriptures never identify him as a seer or a prophet. Positioned and set into his ministry office by the Levitical leaders, he was simply a sensitive and able Levite, called to perform a task at a certain time. The serious nature of his task, and the sense of the awesomeness of the vision of God for the song, placed great demands upon his gift. But this man wasn't a novice. He was also a capable administrator: Chenaniah is mentioned one last time in 1 Chronicles 26:29, as a judge responsible for the outward affairs of the Temple.

Thoughtfully, Chenaniah considered the forthcoming celebration. God had ordered that the Ark must be carried on long wooden poles, borne on the shoulders of the Levites. The shoulders are representative of authority. The burden of the song of the Lord must be lifted and carried with godly authority. When executed with authority, the song of the Lord commands a response, taking charge of the spiritual atmosphere. Such authoritative leadership establishes the boundaries within which the song is to be ministered. This quality of leadership is not generally an inherent characteristic. Occasionally, leaders capable of godly, authoritative leadership are born. More often, though, this quality is learned through godly example. Over time, it develops into a humble confidence by which the leader is able to direct others without coercion. Chenaniah needed to communicate this feature to the singers. Bearing the burden of the song of the Lord requires a firm, authoritative hand, led of the Spirit, inspired by faith and motivated by love.

Chenaniah was an instructor. He taught the Levites how to corporately bear the burden of the Lord's song. He was a man of experience, able to teach and train. Without that training, the song would sound confused and disjointed. The singers of that day needed to be taught, and so do we.

The Hebrew word for instructor in 1 Chronicles 15:22 is from the verb *yasar*, which means 'to chastise, admonish, correct, instruct and discipline'. Chenaniah's instruction corrected and guided the singers into an orderly fashion of ministry. There had been no such order during the first procession. A chaotic, loud sound had erupted from a sincere and well-meaning people. But good intentions without good instruction result in disastrous endeavours. Ministering the burden of the song of the Lord, therefore, requires tremendous discipline. This discipline sets vital boundaries of self-control, unity and authority.

Chenaniah learned the importance of co-ordinating the ministry of the song of the Lord with the actual carrying of the Ark of God's presence. Bearing the burden of the song meant that Chenaniah was appointed to inspire the singers with a joyful, resounding song of praise.

As the process of restoring the Ark to its rightful place began, with Chenaniah skilfully leading the Levites in song, the significance of this long-awaited moment exploded in Chenaniah's heart and a spirit of faith spread like wildfire through the entire group. As the Levites placed the wooden staves on their shoulders and began to carry the Ark pace by pace, there was a great outburst of jubilant celebration. Mile after mile, the song increased in intensity. David and the leaders of Israel danced wildly. Under Chenaniah's anointed leadership, the burden of the song had been successfully lifted up. This time life resulted instead of death.

11

The Schools of the Prophets

It had been a strange night. Lying on his bed Saul meditated on the unusual situation he found himself in. The
journey had started out so innocently. Greatly frustrated
while attempting to locate some lost animals, he and his
servant had come to Samuel the seer's house, requesting
assistance. Strangely, Samuel appeared to be expecting
him. It was almost as if the lost asses had been a stratagem
arranged by God to guide him to this prophet's quarters.
Long into the night Samuel and he had conversed.
Somehow Samuel already knew about the lost donkeys
and that they had been found. What would this new day
bring? Mysterious possibilities seemed to loom on the
horizon.

After arising, Samuel escorted Saul and his servant to
the edge of the city and then sent the servant on ahead.
Taking a vial of oil, the seer poured the sweet-smelling
contents on Saul's head and kissed him. The words which
he then spoke burned in Saul's trembling heart: Samuel
had just anointed him to be King of Israel. After this,
Samuel prophesied to Saul concerning forthcoming
events; and everything happened just as Samuel foretold.

One of these events involved an amazing new experience for Saul. As he approached the city near to the

Philistine garrison, he heard the sound of an approaching group of prophets who spontaneously prophesied in word and song, accompanied on a variety of instruments. The atmosphere was impregnated by the Spirit of God. Without warning and without human explanation, Saul felt as if he had been vigorously seized in his inner man. His heart raced and words such as he had never heard before began to pour out of his mouth. His tongue was like the pen of a skilled and ready writer, his heart was one with God, enraptured by the same Spirit who moved upon these wandering prophets. It may have lasted for hours or perhaps just a few moments, but no matter what, one thing he knew for sure. He would never be the same again.

In 1 Samuel 10 Saul, the newly anointed King of Israel, encountered a group of prophets who, accompanied by a variety of musical instruments, prophesied in song under the powerful unction and influence of the Spirit of the Lord. Let us look at this situation more closely.

The beginning of the historical schools of the prophets

Samuel arose as a seer and a prophet to Israel in a time when the word of the Lord was rare. Although no more than a child, his God-given calling developed quickly. Revered and trusted, his prophecies were accorded great respect. As he matured, followers began to surround him, desiring to learn of his wisdom and receive an impartation of his spirit. Then, as interest grew, Samuel developed a system whereby these hungry students might learn to function in the same anointing in which he ministered. Hence the school of the prophets began.

Prophetic schools designed in order to practise the principle of impartation

These prophetic schools were constructed on the principle of impartation. Small societies of students seeking to receive a measure of the prophet's anointing gathered around the prophetic leader. As they studied the secret methods of prophetic ministry, these pupils, together with their families, would live together in colonies around their master. An environment such as this created a sort of spiritual incubator, enabling each individual to grow and develop. The impartation occurred as the same anointing of the Spirit that rested upon Samuel moved upon and seized the student. Suddenly the disciple began to prophesy, being literally overcome by God's presence. While in the presence of the prophet, the individual's will was free to praise, worship and prophesy of the Lord. The disciple was overwhelmed by the awesome presence of God; all other matters became insignificant and were forgotten.

In exceptional cases, the Spirit would lay hold on a person who was inwardly hostile to God, as in the case of Saul and his messengers (1 Sam 19). But God seeks for more honourable and willing vessels.

Development of the prophetic training and education process

Years of training were required in the development of the gift. These centres of prophetic growth were cultivated by several methods of education. The prophetic schools of Samuel, Elijah, Elisha and others became the centres for religious life, where communion with God was the emphasis. Through the expressions of prayer, meditation and the recollection of the past mighty works of the Lord, the students prepared themselves to receive inspiration for prophecy and revelation. These principles established the foundations for biblical praise and worship.

In the earliest stages of development the pupils would arouse themselves through the use of music. Inducing a frantic, ecstatic condition, the music would affect the entire group, often resulting in unusual and shocking behaviour. Perhaps at the beginning of these schools this was common. As time progressed, however, an element of wisdom and self-control began to manifest. The extremes of enthusiasm were replaced by sincere desire and wisdom. Sung prophecies, still spontaneous, were carefully written down, and the unusual physical behaviour gradually lessened and eventually ceased. We must be careful not to ignore or reason away the overwhelming effect that the Spirit of God had upon these people if we are to understand these schools.

The ministry of the seer

Samuel, the founder of the prophetic schools, was first identified as a seer in 1 Samuel 9. Numerous other men bore the same title. It appears to have been commonly accepted that the term 'seer' was synonymous with 'prophet' (1 Sam 9:9). In some instances God anointed certain individuals to be the king's personal seer. Gad, Heman and Jeduthun all functioned in such a role.

A seer sees into things that are normally hidden, and hears things that are normally beyond the human ear. Inspired by the spirit of prophecy, the seer would look into something by the Spirit and discover the revelations that God would choose to unfold. At the proper time, the seers would then speak out the word of the Lord in the way which was most effective in that particular situation.

An atmosphere of unity existed in the prophetic schools

Under the direction of Samuel, Elijah and others, the prophetic schools were organised into tightly-knit groups of individuals. When Saul first encountered the group of prophets descending from the high place, he was temporarily caught up in their intensely unified atmosphere. The Hebrew word translated as 'group' can also mean 'a rope, a cord or something tightly twisted together'. Used of the prophets, this word paints the picture of a group so tightly woven together that each of them depended on all the others in order to survive. The body of Christ needs this unified atmosphere and commitment in the prophetic ministry and song.

Purposes of the prophetic schools

The purposes of the prophetic schools were many and various. Let us summarise the main goals.

The first and most important purpose has already been discussed in detail—that is, the training of individuals in the prophetic ministry.

The second purpose was really something of a side effect. The presence of a prophetic school in a particular area exercised a powerful influence on the surrounding neighbourhood. When the prophets sang and prophesied, the people living in the area became more aware of the presence of the Spirit of God than of the activity of Satan. Satanic influence was bound and restricted, so that the people were presented with an opportunity to change and be delivered. Consider the amazing possibilities if the church today would practise this principle. I am not suggesting that the reinstitution of prophetic schools is necessary. But might it be possible for the church to create an atmosphere and embrace an experience similar to that of the schools?

Think of the effect this could have on individual lives and communities. The disciples on the Day of Pentecost had such an effect in Jerusalem when they were empowered by the Spirit to speak the wonderful works of God (Acts 2:1–18).

One of the most constructive means of influencing our cities and nations for God could be this corporate, Spirit-inspired, spontaneous and scriptural manifestation of the prophetic song of the Lord. It is time for the church to wake up and sing a new song under the anointing of the spirit of prophecy which will challenge the unsaved and confront the backslider with the undeniable presence of God.

12

Various Types of Prophetic Song

Every gardener knows that if you plant carrot seeds, you'll reap a harvest of carrots. God ordained from the creation of the world that every seed would yield fruit after its own kind (Gen 1:11–12). This is both a natural and a spiritual law. Each type of fruit tree brings forth fruit according to the type of tree it is. Apple trees naturally bring forth apples. They don't and can't produce oranges. Using this natural principle as an analogy, Jesus compared the prophetic ministry to a fruit tree (Mt 7:15–20). The false prophets will bear corrupt fruit and the godly prophets will yield good fruit. Jesus cautions the believer to learn to distinguish and judge the fruit in order to discern the nature of prophetic ministry.

Now, let's go one step further. As already illustrated, apple trees grow apples, orange trees grow oranges, and pear trees produce pears. Just as there are countless different types of fruit tree, each bearing a fruit after its own kind, so there are countless types of prophet and each will bring forth fruit that is according to the calling and assignment God has given him. Therefore, certain types of prophet will sing specific types of prophetic song according to the type of 'fruit tree' they are called to be.

Some of the most common types of prophet identified in the Scriptures

The following is a list of some of the many different types of prophet God has planted on the earth. Because of the manifold nature of God's grace and callings, this list cannot be complete; God has a way of making every person so unique that no individual minister will be identical to another.

Prophets to a nation or nations

'Before I formed you in the womb I knew you; before you were born I sanctified you; I ordained you a prophet to the nations' (Jer 1:5).

Prophets responsible for certain territorial areas, cities, churches or regions

This can include those individuals called to be a prophet to certain cultures and groups of people in a generation. 'Now the word of the Lord came to Jonah the son of Amittai, saying, "Arise, go to Nineveh, that great city, and cry out against it; for their wickedness has come up before Me"' (Jon 1:1–2).

Prophets to an individual minister—generally a king, leader or another prophet

Gad—David's personal seer: 'Now when David arose in the morning, the word of the Lord came to the prophet Gad, David's seer, saying . . .' (2 Sam 24:11).

Heman–David's personal seer:—'All these were the sons of Heman the king's seer in the words of God, to exalt his horn' (1 Chron 25:5).

Juduthun—the king's personal seer: 'And the singers, the sons of Asaph, were in their places, according to the command of David, Asaph, Heman, and Jeduthun the king's seer' (2 Chron 35:15).

Aaron, prophet to Moses: 'So the Lord said to Moses: "See, I have made you as God to Pharaoh, and Aaron your brother shall be your prophet"' (Exod 7:1).

Prophets in training, sons of the prophets

'And the sons of the prophets who were at Bethel came out to Elisha, and said to him, "Do you know that the Lord will take away your master from over you today?"' (2 Kings 2:3).

'And Saul sent messengers to take David: and when they saw the company of the prophets prophesying, and Samuel standing as appointed over them, the spirit of God was upon the messengers of Saul, and they also prophesied' (1 Sam 19:20, KJV).

Prophets who function as shepherds or pastorally

'As for me, I have not hurried away from being a shepherd who follows You, nor have I desired the woeful day; You know what came out of my lips; it was right there before You' (Jer 17:16).

Prophets who are like mothers and fathers to other prophets

As with Elijah to Elisha: 'Then it happened, as they continued on and talked, that suddenly a chariot of fire appeared with horses of fire, and separated the two of them; and Elijah went up by a whirlwind into heaven. Now Elisha saw it, and he cried out, "My father, my father, the chariot of Israel and its horsemen!" So he saw him no more. And he took hold of his own clothes and tore them into two pieces' (2 Kings 2:11–12).

Prophetic elders

As in the case of Judas and Silas: 'Then it pleased the apostles and elders, with the whole church, to send chosen men
of their own company to Antioch with Paul and Barnabas,
namely, Judas who was also named Barsabas, and Silas,
leading men among the brethren . . . Now Judas and Silas,
themselves being prophets also, exhorted and strengthened the brethren with many words' (Acts 15:22; 32).

Judas and Silas are examples of prophets whose ministry was combined with another of the five ministry
offices mentioned in Ephesians 4:11, such as the apostolic
or teaching office. In this case the prophetic calling was
more predominant than the apostolic office.

Prophetesses

Miriam: 'Then Miriam the prophetess, the sister of Aaron,
took the timbrel in her hand; and all the women went out
after her with timbrels and with dances' (Exod 15:20).

Deborah: 'Now Deborah, a prophetess, the wife of
Lapidoth, was judging Israel at that time' (Judg 4:4).

*The prophetic song sung by the believer not necessarily called
to the office of prophet but desiring to move in the gift of
prophecy*

'Pursue love, and desire spiritual gifts, but especially that
you may prophesy' (1 Cor 14:1).

False prophets, or those who prophesy out of their own spirit

For example, the prophets of Baal and the groves (1 Kings
18:18–19, KJV).

Each prophetic minister is unique

We can learn from the variety demonstrated in the
above list. Each type of prophet had a different degree of

authority and grace and a different purpose, which defined the areas in which their ministry was to be exercised. Normally their ministry would be confined to these areas, though on occasion God might call them to minister in different areas. These prophets prophesied and sang their inspired songs as the Spirit of the Lord willed on each occasion.

Notice too that prophetic song is not confined to those who are called to the prophetic office described in Ephesians 4:11; however, in the case of those who are so called, the anointing and fluency of the song will tend to be greater. It's good to recognise the measure of gifting which God has given us. Remember also that some individuals are called to more than one ministry office; and most importantly that they are called by God. Man cannot appoint himself to such a position.

Let us look more closely at some scriptural examples.

The prophetic ministry of Jeremiah

The prophetic poems, songs and messages of Jeremiah were directed to the nations and also dealt with any person or circumstance which would affect the nations to which he was appointed. Ezekiel, Amos and many of the Minor Prophets delivered similar prophetic songs. Their messages consistently targeted the leadership and condition of the nations. Their prophecies were composed of intercessions, prayers, praise and even spiritual warfare. These prophets seldom ministered to individual needs unless those individuals were leaders or up-and-coming leaders.

The prophetic ministry of Habakkuk

Habakkuk's prophecy was addressed to the conflict between Babylon and Israel. His intercessory song in chapter 3 speaks prophetically of Israel and the church opposing Babylon in the Last Days. The time may be approaching when we will be forced to sing that prophetic song of Habakkuk once again. Is today's church prepared for the struggle?

The prophetic ministries of Gad, Heman and Jeduthun

The prophetic songs of Gad, Heman and Jeduthun were different. Although many of their songs emphasised praise and worship, these men functioned particularly as David's personal prophets. It is possible that many of their songs were for David alone. David was able to receive from their ministry because he trusted them. They had proved themselves throughout years of service and relationship.

The prophetic ministry of Deborah

The Book of Judges is a fascinating and inspiring account. It is one of the few books in the Scriptures that really teach about revival! The children of Israel were constantly needing revival. Backsliding and falling into idolatry, turning away from God again and again, they were perpetually needing his delivering hand and restoration. Their sins continually brought the judgement of God down upon them. Only when their enemies oppressed them would Israel cry out in repentance, pleading for mercy and deliverance. Ehud, Othniel, Gideon, Jepthah—all mighty men of God—were anointed by God to set the Children of Israel free and restore them. These men were revivalists. In this chronicle of leaders there is one who is unique in having left behind one of the finest examples of prophetic and poetic song ever recorded in the Scriptures. Her name was Deborah.

Deborah was indeed a unique woman. God raised her

up in a role which had been traditionally occupied by men, anointing her as a revivalist, a prophetess and a warrior. Though she is referred to as a 'mother in Israel' (Judg 5:7), there is no record of her being the mother of natural children. Her children were those whom she capably governed and parented. She was revered and honoured by the people of Israel who regularly sought her advice as she declared the wise counsel of God while sitting beneath the palm tree bearing her name (Judg 4:5). As a judge to Israel, she ruled with equity a land free from war and bondage for forty years.

Occasionally such a woman as Deborah will impact human lives and events during times of national oppression and despair. More than a prophetess, she aroused the broken and fearful nation from a state of apathy and hopelessness to animate themselves for war. She instilled in them a warrior's heart and a determination to be free from the Canaanites who were oppressing them. Words, however, were not her only weapon. Sending for Barak, a descendent of the tribe of Naphtali, she prophetically charged him with the awesome responsibility of leading Israel and delivering the land from its enemies. Barak refused to fight such a formidable foe unless Deborah went with him. Undaunted, she agreed to go. Facing tremendous odds and aided by Deborah's fearless, warrior anointing, Barak defeated the Canaanite general Sisera and his mighty army.

This miraculous victory inspired Deborah's prophetic song of the Lord, which is regarded as one of the finest examples of ancient Hebrew poetry (Judg 5). In magnificent language it declares the supernatural truth which lay behind the outcome of the battle against Sisera: 'The Lord came down for me against the mighty' (Judg 5:13). Sisera's great army and iron chariots were no match for the might of God. This is a song we will no doubt hear again before the Lord returns. The body of Christ must lift up a resounding voice as Deborah did, and call itself to awake and sing!

The prophetic songs of the believer will flow forth out of the grace, authority and calling which they have been granted. However, let us take care that in our zeal to be used by God we do not unthinkingly step outside the boundaries of our anointing, thereby grieving the Spirit. May love, faith and grace keep us from doing so.

The prophetic heart of Abel

Abel is identified in Luke 11:49–51 as the first prophet. There is no record of him having sung, but had he done so his songs would undoubtedly have possessed a prophetic essence. Murdered by the hand of Cain, his brother, over the issue of acceptable worship, Abel's prophetic heart and voice were silenced. The way of Cain still exists today unfortunately. People like Cain, driven by dead works, jealous of others and ignoring God's prophetic order in worship, continually attempt to kill and silence the song of the Lord. But the matter is not hopeless. In merciful kindness God gave another son to Adam and Eve, named Seth. Seth's name appropriately means 'a substitute'. God will not allow the prophetic trees to die. Job 14:7–9 says it well: 'For there is hope for a tree, if it is cut down, that it will sprout again, and that its tender shoots will not cease. Though its root may grow old in the earth, and its stump may die in the ground, yet at the scent of water it will bud and bring forth branches like a plant.'

Even though the prophetic tree is often felled, the song will grow again. The slightest scent of spiritual water revives it. It's hard to keep a good tree down.

13

The Purpose of Prophetic Song

To everything there is a purpose and the prophetic song is no different. The Bible indicates that it has in fact several distinct purposes, which are edification, exhortation, comfort, instruction and occasionally direction for the future: 'But he who prophesies speaks edification and exhortation and comfort to men' (1 Cor 14:3).

The purpose of edification is discussed in detail in a separate chapter.

The purpose of exhortation

Exhortation is the act of encouraging people to increase in faith and virtue. Paul speaks of his preaching the gospel as an exhortation. Prophecy is a special means of exhortation. In Acts 4:36, Barnabas is called the Son of Encouragement, referring to his prophetic gift manifested especially in encouraging others. Encouragement was also expressed in his lifestyle: 'And Joses, who was also named Barnabas by the apostles (which is translated Son of Encouragement), a Levite of the country of Cyprus, having land, sold it, and brought the money and laid it at the apostles' feet' (Acts 4:36–37).

Barnabas understood the principles of exhortation. In

order to exhort, one has to thrive on giving encouragement. Exhortation could aptly be compared to the launching power of rocket engine jets. Unmotivated, passive Christians are waiting for that surge of confident power to be released in their lives through the explosive force of exhortation. Barnabas was openly recognised for his ability to do this. But Barnabas was also a prophet. His unique prophetic style unlocked the doors of opportunity for the apostle Paul. Believing in Paul's calling, Barnabas encouraged him and stood as a willing advocate on Paul's behalf before the Jerusalem apostles and leaders. His example is a wonderful model for us today.

The words of the prophetic song of exhortation and the manner of its delivery are full of a spirit of faith, inspiring faith and hope where previously these were lacking. What an amazing tool!

Prophecy must find its foundations in the Scriptures

All true prophecy has its foundation in the Scriptures. Without the truths of God's word, the song of exhortation results in emotional hype and false hope. Participants in New Age religions have created a counterfeit of true exhortation, which produces a false self-confidence without God. The body of Christ is in danger of falling into the same snare. Without realising it, Christians may attempt to sing an exhortation in prophecy which is based on emotion rather than scriptural truth. Genuine hope is produced only by exhortation based on God's word.

The prophetic song of exhortation lovingly encourages upright living

Prophetic song which exhorts the believer encourages the individual towards virtue and moral uprightness. As God chastens his people, the prophetic song strengthens the needy soul, with faith and courage, enabling the Christian to overcome sin. The forthright words of the exhortation, with a surgeon's skill, cut away the excuses of the carnal nature and press home the truth. But this must always be tempered by love.

Exhortation must be free from deceit

Another characteristic of exhortation is the strength and forcefulness of its message. For this reason it can make a powerful impact on the heart of the listener. Unfortunately, this also makes it possible for exhortation to be abused for manipulative, ungodly purposes. Therefore the ministry of such prophetic song must be scrutinised under the microscope of biblical truth to determine the genuine motivations of the minister.

The apostle Paul illustrated that he was always careful to maintain a ministry of exhortation which was free from deceit. Paul and his associates had encountered a degree of resistance towards their ministry in the church at Thessalonica. At times such as this, Paul faced a temptation that can ensnare the best of ministers. Desiring to woo the hesitant hearts in the church, Paul could have masterfully juggled his exhortative words in an attempt to sway the opinion of the Thessalonican believers. He didn't, however, stoop to such ungodly behaviour. Instead of using flattery and unrealistic promises, he spoke the truth and conveyed the love of God. His heart and motives were pure. (See 1 Thessalonians 2:2–8.) Ungodly exhortation seeks to exalt the self. It is covetous and loves the praises of men more than the praises of God; it is coarse and rudely ministered.

Genuine exhortation in prophetic song is as gentle as the very nature of the Holy Spirit. It corrects without crushing and is then able to impart the very nature of the soul of the one ministering the song. Through the prophetic song of exhortation, the graces and abilities of God are multiplied in the believer.

The church is in desperate need of this song. Without it, the body of Christ will wither and decrease. People need the strength which this song will inject into their hearts. Whenever this song manifests, the church grows and multiplies.

The purpose of comfort

Another purpose of prophetic song is comfort. God is the God of all comfort. Every type of comfort originates with him. Once having been comforted by God, the Christian is able to sing prophetically out of an understanding heart to those in need. In 1 Thessalonians 2:11, Paul compares this comfort to the tender ministry of a father to his children. This comforting in the song of prophecy ministers a form of consolation which gets close to the heart on an intimate and personal manner and is ministered with a greater degree of tenderness than exhortation. God's Father heart is manifested through this song.

Such an endeavour cannot be accomplished through mere sympathy. A shallow head knowledge of the Scriptures is unsatisfactory to meet the need. This prophetic song perceptively uncovers the deepest wounds with the most gentle, tender utterance of the words, strengthening and healing in a manner that no other ministry can achieve. Only the Spirit of God can anoint us to comfort in this sensitive way.

The needs of the Last Days' generation are almost overwhelming. Grief, pain and confusion have bombarded the lives of humankind. But through the prophetic song, the ashes of sorrow are washed away, as the tender words bathe the heavy heart. Lamenting is replaced by a surge of gladness. The spirit of heaviness and depression is cast aside, and the prophetic song clothes the mourning soul with renewed praise.

Paul charged the church of Thessalonica to comfort the feeble-minded (1 Thess 5:14). The Greek word translated feeble-minded is better rendered as 'small-souled, faint-hearted or weak-headed'. Nothing can break through the barrage of thoughts which oppress the human mind more effectively than an appropriately timed, sensitive prophetic song. Clouds of oppressive thoughts are dispelled as the words of the song strengthen the weakened heart. Vision expands as small thinking flees. The prophetic song conveys God's loving concern and heals the weary soul. The body of Christ certainly needs it today.

Our role in ministering comfort through prophetic song

Jacob was devastated when he saw that the many-coloured coat had been torn into shreds and saturated with blood. The owner of the garment was his beloved son, Joseph. His precious, favourite son was dead. One of the most mournful cries of grief ever heard erupted from the depths of his being. For days on end he wept and lamented his dead Joseph. Gathering around their father, Jacob's sons and daughters attempted to comfort their aged father. But he refused their comfort, vowing he would go down into his grave mourning Joseph's death. (See Genesis 37:34–35.)

In order to comfort someone through sung prophecy, the needy soul must possess a desire to be comforted. Receiving comfort is a choice. The walls of hurt must fall. Offering comfort which is wilfully refused by the wounded individual is one of the most frustrating experiences a minister may have. The realistic truth is that not everyone wants to be helped. Failure to acknowledge this fact breeds a sense of discouragement in ministering the song of the Lord. We must remember that we are simply the vessel. He is the Healer. Rejecting the comfort, in reality they reject the Lord's hand. The minister must release the results into the hands of the Lord once a prophetic song is delivered. He is the Great Physician. We're simply his tools.

The purpose of direction

On occasion, the prophetic song will minister a message of direction to the listener. When Agabus prophesied to Paul, the theme of his message wasn't new to Paul. Agabus' prophetic word merely confirmed what Paul already knew by the revelation of the Spirit. This principle of confirmation reigns true throughout the Scriptures. Directional prophetic songs and messages which are unaccompanied by confirmation are dangerous! James said it well: let us be swift to hear and slow to speak (Jas 1:19). The long-term effects of an unwisely delivered directional prophecy can be devastating. Be sensitive, and minister such songs with caution and love.

The purpose of instruction

Lastly, prophecy is given for the purpose of instruction. Prophecy is also defined as inspired preaching and teaching; this may take the form of a prophetic song.

One of the most beautiful manifestations of teaching available to the church is that which is delivered, by inspiration of the spirit of prophecy, in language which has poetic qualities. Equally beautiful is the prophetic song which gives instruction.

No matter what form prophetic song takes, it is destined to be a blessing. Let us grow in the grace of this gift of song, ministering this unique manifestation to the body of Christ.

14

The Spirit of Prophecy

Spiritual things are probably the most difficult matters on earth to explain. Limited as we are in our capacity to understand spiritual manifestations because of our fleshly nature and human thinking, we are constantly striving to learn and understand everything we can. Then, if we can't figure it out, or find it's a spiritual manifestation that is unexplainable, we toss it away. But a great number of the matters of the Spirit cannot be explained easily, and some things aren't meant to be until God sees fit. The Scriptures are our only source of absolute truth in this conflict.

For years I have wanted to be able to explain the operation and manifestation of God's Spirit in the spirit of prophecy. I am well aware that perceptions, experiences and feelings are far from adequate. This is a difficult subject to handle, but in order to learn to minister the song of the Lord in a prophetic sense, some sort of teaching is desirable. Fortunately, the Bible does indicate a certain pattern concerning the function of the spirit of prophecy in the believer's life.

The spirit of prophecy is the testimony of Jesus

The apostle John relates one of the most important principles concerning the spirit of prophecy in Revelation

19:10—'And I fell at his feet to worship him. But he said to me, "See that you do not do that! I am your fellow servant, and of your brethren who have the testimony of Jesus. Worship God! For the testimony of Jesus is the spirit of prophecy."' Everything that Jesus accomplished in his death and resurrection is the essence and origin of prophecy. Without the remembrance of the cross, the shedding of his precious blood and the triumphant resurrection as he destroyed the works of the devil, prophecy is empty. The power of the spirit of prophecy is located in this knowledge.

As Jesus laid his own life down, so must those who yearn to prophesy. Until we desire to see his life shining through us, our prophecy will be shallow and futile. The equipping power of the Spirit is found in the humility of acknowledging Jesus' lordship. God is near to those who are broken and contrite in heart and who recognise that without him we are nothing, but that in him we are more than conquerors. When this happens, the power of God's Spirit literally overcomes the believer, compelling him to see or hear things which otherwise would be hidden.

Several examples can be noted and will help explain how God's Spirit manifests in this to the Christian.

Manifestations of the spirit of prophecy in the life of the individual minister

The Spirit compared to a garment

'And the Spirit of God came upon him' is the most common phrase describing the operation of the spirit of prophecy. Like a garment, the spirit of prophecy clothed the individual with God's power to prophesy. In

1 Chronicles 12:18, the Spirit came upon Amasai: 'Then the Spirit came upon Amasai, chief of the captains, and he said: "We are yours, O David; we are on your side, O son of Jesse! Peace, peace to you, and peace to your helpers! For your God helps you." So David received them, and made them captains of the troop.' According to C. Von Orrelli, a contributing author on the subject of prophecy in *The International Standard Bible Encyclopedia*, vol. IV, a better translation of this phrase would be 'the Spirit clothed Amasai'.

This demonstration of the spirit of prophecy is difficult to describe. It's an almost tangible experience as, like an unseen garment, the presence of God embraces the individual.

The Spirit falls upon the individual

In several instances it is stated that the Spirit of the Lord *fell* upon the individual: 'Then the Spirit of the Lord fell upon me, and said to me, "Speak! 'Thus says the Lord: "Thus you have said, O house of Israel; for I know the things that come into your mind"'"' (Ezek 11:5).

Ezekiel's experience of the Spirit was often of an overwhelming nature and he gives several accounts of it; for example: 'So the Spirit lifted me up and took me away, and I went in bitterness, in the heat of my spirit; but the hand of the Lord was strong upon me' (Ezek 3:14).

Authority is granted

Notice that Ezekiel also describes his experience as the hand of the Lord being upon him. The Jews, when speaking of the hand, were often symbolically referring to authority. Therefore, to speak of the hand of the Lord was to speak of the authority of the Lord. When the spirit of prophecy falls in this way an incredible sense of authority and strength is granted. The prophet Ezra experienced this impartation of strength as mentioned in Ezra 7:28: 'And hath extended mercy unto me before the king, and his counsellors, and before all the king's mighty princes. And I was strengthened as the hand of the Lord my God was upon me, and I gathered together out of Israel chief men to go up with me' (KJV).

Most of the time it seems today's Christian will not in fact experience the more radical manifestations mentioned here, though it is important to know what the Bible says about them. Today, God is most likely to use the more common and established methods in which to speak to the believer, such as his word and the inward witness, which we shall consider later.

The spirit of prophecy does not suppress the human consciousness

The spirit of prophecy does not suppress the human consciousness of the believer, who is able afterwards to give a clear account of what has happened. Rather, as the Spirit of God ministers to the individual, his or her awareness of the things of the Spirit of God is acutely changed, as if for a moment the mind is more aware of God than of the immediate surroundings; the individual *co-operates* with God in the formal shaping of that which has been seen or heard.

An exalted poetical language may emerge

Throughout the Scriptures, the utterances of an inspired prophet or speaker are frequently marked by an exalted and poetical language. This lyrical gift will often assume a rhythmical character, not bound by narrow or mechanical metre but flowing like the waters in a mountain stream. These words are not a product of the speaker's own spirit; they are like seeds planted by God in the heart of the receiver.

Isaiah indicated that he even saw the words of the prophecy with the eyes of his heart: 'The word that Isaiah the son of Amoz saw concerning Judah and Jerusalem' (Is 2:1).

Divine certainty enters the soul of the recipient

True prophecy does not originate out of the individual's personal reflections, feelings, fears or hopes. With the spirit of prophecy there comes to the believer a divine certainty. Without a shadow of doubt they *know* that God has spoken to them. From the first moments of this visitation the believer will most commonly regard the inspiration with fear and trembling, coupled with a sense of absolute compulsion to speak. Until they are uttered, the words literally burn within the soul.

Observations of wisdom are different from prophecy

At this point it is necessary to distinguish wisdom from inspired prophecy. Wisdom is accumulated through observation, research and understanding, while prophecy is actually inspired by the spirit of prophecy. Both are vital to the ministry of God's word but we need to make certain that we note the difference between them. Prophecy occurs because God has spoken. It is a serious matter to say to others, 'God has told me . . .', so we must be careful not to mistake a wise observation for a prophecy. Of course, this is not to deny the value of speaking forth wisdom. On some occasions, after wisdom has pinpointed an issue, God will speak prophetically. But let's learn to make the distinction.

Anyone claiming to have received the spirit of prophecy must also be able to distinguish the content of the revelation from his own thoughts and knowledge. This takes time and patience. If God has genuinely spoken, his word will confirm it.

The spirits of the prophets are subject to the prophets

Personal factors can condition the way in which the prophet gives expression to his word from God. Paul wrote to the church of Corinth about this very issue. In 1 Corinthians 14:32 Paul states that the spirits of the prophets are subject to the control of the prophets. This implies that every inspired utterance will probably be interpreted by the recipient according to their past experiences (good or bad), their personal doctrines (right or wrong), their desires and fears, their talents and their personality. Therefore, when a prophecy is given, it must first be tested by the Scripture. But after that it must also be tested in order to determine whether, and in what way, it has been influenced by the predispositions of the speaker. Just because someone says that God spoke to them, doesn't mean it's always so.

Pieces of a massive puzzle

Prophecies are like single pieces of a massive puzzle. In most instances, God will not give us the entire picture. While they were alone in prayer, the spirit of prophecy would fall upon the prophets of old. Usually they didn't understand everything they had seen. Daniel puzzled over some of these revelations for weeks at a time. If these messages are to be understood and accurately delivered, wisdom and patient waiting are required. We know in part and consequently we prophesy in part (1 Cor 13:9).

The spirit of prophecy seeks to edify

Prophecy edifies the church. Edification is built on the foundation of love. Without love, the prophetic song is just a bunch of noisy, clanging cymbals. I have observed that in church situations where the spirit of prophecy is allowed to manifest, chaos may result if the principle of edification isn't considered. Those who have the gift of prophecy can become reckless and this creates problems. Owing to the receptivity of those desiring to be used by the Lord, almost any person present may begin to receive some word or song from the Lord and unfortunately, unless they have understanding of this manifestation, they may feel bound to deliver it. This frequently produces needless repetition. On occasion such repetition isn't harmful and can even be helpful in confirming that everyone is hearing the same thing. But receiving a song or prophecy doesn't always mean that we are required to deliver it. This dilemma can be solved quite simply. Whom does the song of prophecy most edify—the individual or the assembly?

> Pursue love, and desire spiritual gifts, but especially that you may prophesy. For he who speaks in a tongue does not speak to men but to God, for no one understands him; however, in the spirit he speaks mysteries. But he who prophesies speaks edification and exhortation and comfort to men. He who speaks in a tongue edifies himself, but he who prophesies edifies the church (1 Cor 14:1–4).

Yielding to the spirit of prophecy means being willing to say, 'I missed it!'

No one enjoys being wrong. Yet one of the finest virtues any Christian can hope to have is the ability to say, 'I missed it.' The prophet doesn't speak at all times in an inspired state. Nathan was compelled to take back a word he had spoken on his own authority when, before the Lord had spoken to him, he encouraged David to proceed with the building of the Temple (2 Sam 7:1–17).

For this reason, the believer must allow all prophecies to be examined and judged. We are on the edge of the chasm of deception if we can't admit that we might be wrong. No one possesses all revelation. We're all growing, subject to various elements which affect our accuracy, our sensitivity and our ability to express things. Rather than condemning one another, or even ourselves, we must be willing to learn, grow and even fail if necessary. The only one who knows it all is God!

Doors through which the spirit of prophecy enters

Like unseen open doors, there are several conditions which promote the release of God's Spirit in the song of prophecy.

The door of desire

Paul instructed the church of Corinth in 1 Corinthians 14:1 to desire spiritual gifts, especially the gift of prophecy. Later, in the same chapter, he went on to say that they should covet to prophesy (1 Cor 14:39, KJV). The covetousness Paul was referring to was an extremely intense desire, based upon the personal relationship one has with Christ. There is also an ungodly covetousness: in

Colossians 3:5 Paul compares covetousness to idolatry and strongly condemns it. This covetousness is entirely different from the coveting to prophesy which Paul urges the believers at Corinth to practise.

When the motivation of the heart is contrary to the peace of God, a proper desire is replaced by ungodly covetousness, fostering a ministry born of lust and always greedy for more. Competing with other believers and comparing themselves with others, those motivated by such passions may even covet another person's prophetic calling and ability to sing prophecy. Jesus cannot be Lord in the lives of people who thus idolise ministry and spiritual manifestations.

The door of the will of the Spirit

However earnest our desire for the outpouring of the spirit of prophecy, we must recognise that it is a gift given as God wills. It is also given when he wills; the believer should not attempt to prophesy at any time he chooses. Such behaviour is in direct conflict with the sovereignty of God. God is the giver of all good and perfect gifts and our will must be continually submitted to his. When believers think that they can prophesy at will, the so-called prophetic songs are manufactured out of human desire instead of being born by the inspiration of the Spirit of God. Properly understood, an earnest desire to be used in prophecy is an expression of willingness to co-operate with God's Spirit, his timing and his plan.

According to 1 Corinthians 12:8–11, it is the Spirit who gives the gifts, distributing to every believer as he sees fit. He knows our hearts and is fully aware of what we can and cannot be trusted with. The gift of prophecy in the wrong hands is a dangerous tool. Genuine prophecy ushered in by the will of the Spirit is a blessing.

The door of impartation

> For I long to see you, that I may impart to you some spiritual
> gift, so that you may be established—that is, that I may be
> encouraged together with you by the mutual faith both of
> you and me (Rom 1:11–12).

As a father to many churches and individual Christians,
Paul the apostle longed to see the believers grow. This
gifted man unselfishly sought for opportunities to
impart to others the grace and gifts with which God had
endowed him. This practice of impartation occurs frequently in the Scriptures. Elijah imparted to Elisha.
Samuel imparted to his students and the various
leaders of the day. Jesus imparted to his disciples, and
the apostles imparted to their followers. This is a vital
means of unlocking graces and gifts within the believer.
Impartation takes place through the ministry of laying-
on of hands and through longstanding, caring relationships.

The door of music

> And Elisha said, 'As the Lord of hosts lives, before whom I
> stand, surely were it not that I regard the presence of
> Jehoshaphat king of Judah, I would not look at you, nor see
> you. But now bring me a musician.' Then it happened, when
> the musician played, that the hand of the Lord came upon
> him (2 Kings 3:14–15).

The kings of Israel, Judah and Edom gathered together
discussing the situation facing them. War was imminent.
The King of Moab had rebelled against Israel. King
Jehoshaphat, wishing to know the mind of the Lord,
asked for a prophet of God to speak a word to them.
Elisha, having agreed to minister to them, called for a

minstrel. As the minstrel began to play, the Spirit of the Lord came upon Elisha and he began to prophesy.

Sensitively played, anointed music is a mighty tool through which God may pour out his Spirit in the spirit of prophecy. Ordinary music will not do. The minstrel's heart and attitude are crucial to the release of this anointing. Some minstrels play a song of life and joy. Others play a dirge of death, even though beautiful in sound.

Having arrived at the home of Jairus, Jesus challenged the mourning minstrels to believe. The girl was not dead, only asleep. He had come to wake her. They mocked him and he drove them away from the house. Accompanied by only a few, in an atmosphere free from their deathly influence, he raised the little girl from the dead.

Had those minstrels been like the one assisting Elisha, they might have remained and saturated the atmosphere with faith. Instead, their lamenting song was silenced and they were asked to leave. God uses the avenue of music to anoint his ministers with the spirit of prophecy.

The door of relationships in the body of Christ through grace

I've been privileged to work with some very gifted ministers, whom over the years I have come to call my friends. Though we're seldom together, I appreciate the blessed times we've shared in fellowship and ministry. Many of these brothers and sisters are called into established and proven apostolic and prophetic ministries. Over the course of our friendship I have noticed a wonderful pattern develop. Whenever we are together it is almost as if the gift that God has deposited within me is unlocked in a greater measure. Their various ministry gifts and graces act like a key, releasing gifts within me that otherwise would remain silent. Several of these friends have told me of similar experiences of their own.

One particular evening I was scheduled to speak at a home meeting in Seattle, Washington, for a Bible study fellowship. The living room and dining room areas were filled with people. I was seated, with the guitar slung over my shoulder, leading the group in a time of praise and worship. Some way into the praise and worship time, one of our dearest ministry friends came in and sat at the back of the room. He hadn't eaten his supper, so while the rest of us worshipped the Lord, he leaned against the kitchen table munching a sandwich. Now, I realise this all sounds like a very ordinary setting in a relaxed home fellowship, but God had something special in store. Every time my husband and I have had the privilege of ministering with or simply being with this prophetic brother, the gifts within my life explode, like a stick of dynamite.

Minutes later, while we were worshipping the Lord with our eyes closed, I briefly opened my eyes and gazed around the room. Suddenly, as I looked towards where my friend was sitting Jesus appeared, standing next to him. With his hand on my friend's shoulder, the Lord began to speak words of comfort, direction and healing to him. Then the spirit of prophecy came upon me, inspiring a song from the Lord to my friend. When an opening came during the worship, I began to sing the song of the Lord, knowing that it would be an encouragement and confirmation to this brother and others present in the room. At that moment, this brother threw himself off his chair onto the floor, kneeling and crying out to the Lord in praise. Later that evening, after I had finished speaking, my friend shared with us his account of what had happened.

After finishing his sandwich, he had begun to worship the Lord with the rest of the group. Unexpectedly his eyes were opened and Jesus stood alongside him. As the Lord placed his hand upon his shoulder, he heard Jesus speak to him. Desiring confirmation, he prayed, asking the Lord to confirm what was happening. In the same instant that he breathed the last words of his prayer, God gave me the song. The words of the song were exactly the same as those the Lord had spoken to him just moments before. In humble thanksgiving he knelt before the Lord, rejoicing for the confirmation. God is faithful!

What I have just related is not necessarily a common occurrence. Yet I cannot ignore the reality of this unlocking every time I'm gathered with anointed, gracious and loving ministers. Again, such dramatic manifestations are given in accordance with the will of the Spirit for that time. I have learned to appreciate his timing, his Spirit and his body. I am also fully aware that owing to the nature of this experience, some will attempt to analyse and reason it away. How sad that we've boxed God into our theological categories and psychoanalysed his Spirit. Isn't it time to allow God to be God?

We desperately need each other. Each gift and individual, properly joined into the body of Christ, should and will assist and release the gift within other believers. If we would all play our part, the life of the church would be enriched and strengthened. Supremely we need Jesus, but we need each other too. I'll always be grateful for those believers and ministers who have faith in the gifts that Jesus has given me. Thank God for the door of godly relationships through grace.

15

Songs in the New Testament

The categories of song which are mentioned in the New Testament are different from those which we have identified as songs of the Lord in the Old Testament (apart from the category of the new song, which is mentioned in Revelation 5:9 and 14:3); and the Old Testament term 'song of the Lord' does not occur in the New Testament. However, this does not mean that the song of the Lord is not a valid form of expression today. Though fewer in number, the New Testament types of song, like the Old Testament types, include all forms of praise and worship. The use of psalms by the New Testament church is another point of similarity; as we have seen, various specific types of the song of the Lord are found within the Old Testament Psalter.

Psalms are one of the three main types of song mentioned in the New Testament; the others are hymns and spiritual songs. These categories are given in Colossians 3:16 and Ephesians 5:19: 'Let the word of Christ dwell in you richly in all wisdom, teaching and admonishing one another in psalms and hymns and spiritual songs, singing with grace in your hearts to the Lord' (Col 3:16); '. . . be filled with the Spirit, speaking to one another in psalms and hymns and spiritual songs, making melody in your heart to the Lord' (Eph 5:18–19). It would seem that these are the New Testament forms of the song of the Lord.

When these types of song are manifested, it is extremely difficult to distinguish between them as they overlap with and complement each other. None the less, I should like to try to provide a degree of definition in the hope that some of the confusion may be resolved. The following definitions are not offered in any spirit of dogmatism and I would ask the reader to bear this in mind when considering them, and to maintain a flexible approach.

Psalms

There is a considerable difference between the use of psalms in Old Testament and New Testament situations. In the former, psalms were used as the prayer book and song book of the daily, regular worship and Temple ceremony. The Old Testament psalms were incorporated into the life of the New Testament church but these were not the only psalms in evidence in the early church. At Corinth, the New Testament expression of psalms was seen as being inspired and was not restricted by the structure within which the Old Testament ministry of psalms operated.

'Psalm' is defined as a poem that is set to music, being either chanted or sung with a musical accompaniment or *a cappella*. Like present-day choruses, they were used in private and corporate worship. New Testament believers were encouraged to use them in their personal devotions as the Spirit of God led and the word of God indwelt their hearts, revealing Jesus. Such psalms, in the form of the song of the Lord, do not come from head knowledge. They are composed from a continual fresh revelation of Christ and may include all types of prayer, praise, prophecy, intercession, worship and declaration.

A unique feature of the New Testament psalms is that they are spoken of alongside teaching, tongues, revelations and interpretations. Definitely the result of the inspiration of the Spirit of God, psalms were used in the corporate gathering as a tool for teaching, admonishing and training the body of Christ. As the believers would take turns in singing out, others would listen and be taught. Ephesians 5:19 describes this as a conversational form of ministry and an evidence of being filled with the Spirit. Psalms, therefore, could be one of the greatest tools for bringing unity to the body of Christ provided the principle of edification is embraced.

On occasion this expression may occur spontaneously. Spontaneity, however, does not always mean that it is spiritually accurate and godly. In 1 Corinthians 14:26 the believer is given wise instruction in the ministry of the psalm in the corporate assembly: 'How is it then, brethren? Whenever you come together, each of you has a psalm, has a teaching, has a tongue, has a revelation, has an interpretation. Let all things be done for edification.'

When the believers of Corinth gathered together, they were instructed to come prepared, having already received the psalm beforehand. There was an element of peaceful order in the ministry of the psalm. The purpose of preparation is clear; it allowed motives, accuracy, heart attitude and timing to be considered so that the psalm could indeed be edifying to the whole church. Some feel that in order for something to be spiritual it has to be spontaneous, when in fact this is contrary to the truth. I have known some people become extremely angry when they were asked to abide by these scriptural boundaries, demanding their rights to liberty. Yet God has called us to use our liberty with wisdom and love. Liberty is indeed one of our greatest spiritual blessings but we are required to use it responsibly and not as a cloak for selfish demands. These boundaries, set by the Scriptures, prevent unnecessary babbling, incomplete messages built on limited revelation, inaccurate ministry, selfish ambitions, and chaotic confusion. God is the God of peace, not of confusion. It's a sad sight to see a church in confusion as a result of failing to observe these boundaries of wisdom. Much damage could be prevented if these basic rules of operation were applied.

Spontaneous psalms are best used in the individual's personal devotional times, as a way of releasing the internal fountains. This is also where psalms for the corporate gathering are born and prepared. In Colossians 3:16 and Ephesians 5:18–19, Paul encouraged believers to sing out of their continual experience of Christ and of the Spirit. Psalms and hymns and spiritual songs can all become stale unless we continually draw fresh water from the wells of our hearts.

Martin J. Wyngaarden, in a section on 'Psalms and Christian Liturgy' in *The International Bible Encyclopedia*, suggests that Paul was also addressing a problem in the churches at Ephesus and Colosse. These churches were becoming so dependent on spontaneous psalms that the ancient Psalter was being neglected. Paul's instructions to them included encouraging them to be sensitive to the Spirit leading them in the use of both types of psalm.

Proverbs states that the merry heart does good like a medicine. Psalms are one of the fruits of a merry heart. There is something contagious about the genuine joy of the Lord. James 5:13 indicates that those individuals who are merry should be allowed to sing psalms. When the boundaries of operation are kept in mind, psalms that are inspired by joy and established upon truth will bless the heart of the church.

Hymns

As I have indicated, it is very difficult to distinguish between hymns and psalms, because their functions are so very similar. A hymn may be defined as a previously recorded religious song which celebrates the present and past victories of God. Hymns are frequently a collection of psalms fitted together. The present-day church identifies certain songs as hymns. These songs may or may not include the songs the Scriptures define as hymns. We must be flexible when defining these terms.

Elizabeth's song to Mary is one of the earliest hymns of the New Testament. Mary's response, bearing a remarkable similarity to Hannah's song in 1 Samuel 2, is another great hymn. Zacharias, father of John the Baptist, sang a hymn after the prophesied birth of his son. Even Jesus sang a hymn before going out to the Mount of Olives. Most probably, what he sang was Psalms 115–118 which were traditionally sung after the Passover meal. It is especially significant that Jesus should have sung Psalm 118 just before he was crucified, as it contains a number of prophecies concerning his sufferings, his resurrection and his exaltation.

The great hymns of the New Testament were born out of solid biblical knowledge, prophetic and accurately ministered. God's word, as it is real in our hearts, must always be the foundation for the song of the Lord.

Probably the most dynamic hymn mentioned in the New Testament is found in Acts 16:23–28, a passage which chronicles a remarkable usage of the hymn.

Paul and Silas were in the lowest, darkest and filthiest hold of the prison. They'd been beaten, accused and tortured. They were shackled and bound, sitting in human refuse, weary from the merciless persecution. Yet in their seemingly bleakest hour, at midnight, they started to pray and sing hymns to God. The leading idea of the Greek word for hymn in verse 25 (*hymnos*) is that of praise. There, in that torturous environment, Paul and Silas stirred themselves to prayer and the singing of praise. As they sang about the past victories of God, faith began to soar above their circumstances. We have no record as to what hymns they sang. But sing they did! Suddenly, a great earthquake shook the prison to its foundations; the cell doors flew open and every chain was loosed. This mighty event resulted in the salvation of many souls, including the jailer and his entire family. God had responded to the faith sung in the hymns of Paul and Silas and had broken both physical and spiritual chains.

As we approach the midnight hour of history, great hymns of the past and present will once again resound. A body of Christ, bound in chains and darkness, is about to rise from sleep and sing as it has never sung before. God will shake everything that can be shaken as we sing these hymns of celebration. The last enemies are about to be confronted as God arises in the celebration of the church.

Hymns are a powerful tool in the songs of the Lord. Nevertheless, tools must be used with wisdom. There are scriptural guidelines for using this song of the Lord.

According to Ephesians 5:19 and Colossians 3:16, hymns are to be sung corporately as well as individually. These songs of the Lord are previously written and are therefore not spontaneous—which is not to say that they can't be sung as a song of the Lord. In fact, they are a powerful instrument when precisely timed by the leading of God's Spirit. This song of the Lord is one aspect of what is meant by singing with the understanding. An ordinary song of praise is transformed into an extraordinary song of the Lord when it is inspired by the Holy Spirit's leading and sung in a unified voice by the congregation.

Hymns, like the psalms, are capable of teaching and admonishing the listener. Anointed and inspired by the Spirit, hymns resemble the deep still pools of water on a secluded river shoreline. They are like a reservoir of yesterday's victories, a vast supply of eternal truth. Truth upon truth, psalm upon psalm, hymns are constructed and remind the church of God's sovereign delivering hand. Yet, once born they can become stale unless inspired by the Holy Spirit's prompting.

Hymns are designed to edify and they are probably the most powerful means of doing so in the whole church. Great songs identified by the present-day church as the hymns of yesteryear, have been cast aside as refuse; their message discarded as irrelevant to today's society. But when these noble testimonies are revived under the Holy Spirit's anointing, the entire church is edified. Elderly saints, unfamiliar with all of the modern styles of music, miss the profound truths that these songs offer and are encouraged when the Spirit leads the singing of hymns. Young Christians, ignorant of their vast heritage, stand amazed and challenged by the intensity of their message and the beauty of their melody.

God will restore this marvellous expression of his song as we approach the midnight hour of time. Let everything which can be shaken, shake!

Spiritual songs

The last category of the New Testament song of the Lord is the spiritual song. Spiritual songs comprise all forms of sung prophecy, word of wisdom, word of knowledge and tongues, with the interpretation of those tongues and new songs. In short, spiritual songs are songs inspired directly by the Spirit of God. They are generally spontaneous in nature; their language is that of lyric poetry and they may be accompanied or *a cappella*.

This type of New Testament song of the Lord produces the greatest challenge, owing to the variety of its expression. Consequently, wise boundaries of operation need to be determined. This should be done in a way which avoids creating bondage, yet sets out practical methods for this ministry and its limitations.

Singing in tongues

Paul identified two different classifications in describing singing in 1 Corinthians 14:15—the songs which are sung with the spirit (that is, in tongues) and the songs which are sung with the understanding. Spiritual songs can occur in both categories. Such a situation creates certain problems. Without adequate training in understanding these two types of spiritual song, wisdom flies out of the window, replaced by the thrill of perpetual experience. This doesn't have to be so.

Singing in tongues is the most important and foundational spiritual song mentioned in the Scriptures. Every locked door needs a key. Tongues are one of the most important keys of the Spirit, and they unlock the entrance into the songs of the Spirit. In reality, tongues are the key to all the other gifts of the Spirit, due to the fact that they were the first gift of the Spirit released during the outpouring of the Spirit at Pentecost.

The gift of tongues is probably the most controversial manifestation of the Spirit in Christianity today. Perhaps this is because it is responsible for unlocking the mysteries of God for the believer. Satan therefore hates the gift of tongues and will do anything to stop its usage. And we must be careful not to suppress it ourselves; even the radically extreme Corinthian Church was sternly charged by Paul not to prevent the usage of this controversial gift. Tongues was then and is now a vital gift of the Spirit. But let us look further at what Paul had to say:

> For if I pray in a tongue, my spirit prays, but my understanding is unfruitful. What is the result then? I will pray with the spirit, and I will also pray with the understanding. I will *sing with the spirit*, and I will also *sing with the understanding*. Otherwise, if you bless with the spirit, how will he who occupies the place of the uninformed say 'Amen' at your giving of thanks, since he does not understand what you say? For you indeed give thanks well, but the other is not edified (1 Cor 14:14–17).

Paul encouraged the individual's use of the gift of tongues in ministering the personal expression of the song of the Lord. However, he also advocated that singing in the spirit, or singing in tongues, must also be accompanied by singing with the understanding. It is wise to aim for a balance in the use of both these expressions.

Tongues will operate in different ways in the lives of different believers. Consider this: the Christian may operate in the *gift* of prophecy and yet not be called to the *ministry office* of prophet. These are two similar yet distinct operations of the Spirit. The same distinction applies to tongues, as can be seen from Paul's words in 1 Corinthians 12:27–30:

> Now you are the body of Christ, and members individually. And God has appointed these in the church: first apostles, second prophets, third teachers, after that miracles, then gifts of healings, helps, administrations, varieties of tongues. Are

all apostles? Are all prophets? Are all teachers? Are all workers of miracles? Do all have gifts of healings? Do all speak with tongues? Do all interpret?

These verses list the various ministry offices such as apostle, prophet, teacher and, at the end, the ministry office of tongues. It is clear that not every believer is called to the office of prophet, nor, equally, will every believer function in the ministry office of tongues. Even so, all believers on occasion can prophesy and speak in tongues if they're open to such gifts of the Spirit. Those persons functioning in a ministry office of tongues minister in this gift of the Spirit in a particularly fluent manner.

The general gift of tongues serves several purposes. The individual use of tongues can take place in prayer, praise and personal devotional times. Tongues, which includes singing in tongues, develops the muscles of the human spirit, resulting in personal edification. Faith increases in the believer's heart as they pray, speak and sing in the Spirit or in tongues. 'He who speaks in a tongue edifies himself, but he who prophesies edifies the church' (1 Cor 14:4). 'But you, beloved, building yourselves up on your most holy faith, praying in the Holy Spirit' (Jude 20).

The disciples newly baptised in the Holy Spirit at Pentecost, spoke in tongues. Those who heard them—visitors from other regions—marvelled as they listened to the disciples praising God in the languages of these regions. This corresponds with what Paul indicated: one of the most excellent ways to praise and give thanks is to sing and speak in tongues. Paul went on to say that in doing so, the believer gives thanks well (1 Cor 14:17). This key of singing in tongues can open the door for all other manifestations of the song of the Lord. There are other doors as well, but this marvellous gift of tongues is a unique and supernatural means of yielding to the Spirit of God.

When used in the corporate setting, the gift of tongues ministered by an individual should be interpreted (unless otherwise indicated by the leadership). No one is edified if the tongue isn't interpreted.

As the final hour approaches, the church must put its childish ways behind it. The song of the Lord is not a toy for children to play spiritual games with. It's time to grow up! The New Testament songs of the Lord through psalms, hymns and spiritual songs are destined to become a sign and banner to a dying and lost world. With love as our foundation, we will see God reach the unreachable, touch the untouchable and heal the broken-hearted. As a master conductor, the Lord is waiting for his mighty orchestra and choir to prepare to sing. He's waiting for us. Will we respond as he lifts his baton, and sing?

16

Learning to Listen

Trembling like a leaf, the twelve-year-old boy reflected on his past night's experience. Lying there upon his sleeping mat, Samuel was scared. The awesome encounter had stirred something strangely wonderful in his young heart. God had spoken to him. He meditated on the possibilities, wondering why. What lay ahead for him? God hadn't made himself known for so many years, and now, barely a teenager, he found himself pondering the purpose of the unusual words and vision. Twice God had called his name, 'Samuel, Samuel!' Samuel might never have recognised God's voice and call had Eli not understood what was happening. According to Eli's instruction, Samuel lay quite still and waited until he heard the voice of the Lord call his name a third time. In sincere, childlike faith, he obediently responded and allowed the Lord to speak. Twice before God had called to him, but he hadn't known how to recognise God's voice. No longer ignorant, he could listen and follow his Lord's commands. He would never be the same again. (See 1 Samuel 3.)

Hearing the voice of the Lord—a common but unnecessary struggle

Innumerable Christians struggle with hearing the voice of the Lord. The difficulty that faces them is common in our generation. The problem is not that God isn't speaking but that a great number of believers don't recognise his voice. He *is* speaking, and probably many are truly hearing; others, like Samuel, need to be instructed in recognising God's voice. God's voice should be the most familiar voice we know. But a voice can be familiar only if we have a regular relationship with the one speaking.

Jesus said in John 10:27 that his sheep know his voice: 'My sheep hear My voice, and I know them, and they follow Me.'

There's a precious and intimate relationship awaiting the Christian. We're his sheep and if his word says that we hear him, then that's the truth. Those who continually say that they don't hear God make God a liar, regarding the promise of the Scriptures false. He is speaking, we just haven't taken the time to develop our relationship with him and come to recognise his voice. The Bible has much to say about hearing his voice.

This subject is by far one of the most important stepping stones for the believer seeking to grow in the song of the Lord. Until individuals have learned to hear and recognise God's song sung to them, they'll never fully realise the incredibly marvellous and true joys of praise, worship and prayer. Hearing and recognising God's song to the individual is the foundation for the ministry of the song of the Lord to others. We must learn to recognise his voice and song. We must also repent for every time we've said that we can't hear him or have accused him of not speaking to us. He is true to his word!

Truths from the Scriptures which help us in this matter

He is the one who gives the hearing ear and the seeing eye: 'The hearing ear and the seeing eye, the Lord has made them both' (Prov 20:12). He is the one who opens our ears so that we can hear. Our ears must be awakened from their sleep on a daily basis: 'The Lord God has given Me the tongue of the learned, that I should know how to speak a word in season to him who is weary. He awakens Me morning by morning, he awakens My ear to hear as the learned. The Lord God has opened My ear; and I was not rebellious, nor did I turn away' (Is 50:4–5). We must choose to hear him!

He hasn't left us without help. Our seemingly deaf ears will be opened if we simply pray and ask him to cause us to hear him. David prayed for this and we can too (Ps 143:8). Our prayer must be founded on faith in his word and promises. We must trust that as we pray he'll answer the cry of our heart. Our prayer should be, 'Make me to hear, O Lord!' Following that request we should grate-fully rejoice, saying, 'Thank you for doing it, Lord,' expressing our confidence in his fatherly response. Our attitude should be similar to that of the multitude men-tioned in Luke 5:1. They were desperate to hear Jesus. So desperate that they literally pressed him out into the waters of the Sea of Galilee. When was the last time, through the sincere desire in your heart, that you put pressure on God to speak? God speaks to the Christian who expects and desires him to.

Having prayed, believing that God will speak, it's vital that we understand *how* God speaks. So many Christians are constantly looking for their 'Damascus road' experi-ence, believing that God only speaks through thunder or spectacular signs in the sky. It is impossible to build a solid daily relationship upon such uncommon (though not unscriptural) manifestations. There is no easy way in learning to hear him. It demands a daily relationship with the Lord and a sound understanding of the most common methods by which he speaks to us. It demands discipline and responsibility, which in turn produce obedience.

We can choose to allow him to open our ears, or we can choose to be rebellious and turn away. Hearing God is not just an opportunity. It's a determined and committed choice! If any man has the ears to hear, then he must let himself hear. The human will is linked with the ears of the human spirit. Understanding is the precious fruit of an open, willing, hearing heart.

Seven methods by which God speaks

There are primarily seven methods by which God speaks to his people. They are listed below, beginning with the most common. Not all are used on a regular basis.

Through creation

The first way in which God introduces himself to man is through creation. I am not referring to the idolatrous religions of astrology or pantheism but to the declaration of the existence and glory of the Creator which we see in the vast beauty of creation and the marvels of the starry heavens (see Psalm 19:1–3). Man is without an excuse (Rom 1:20). The continual witness of the greatness of God constantly speaks to the inhabitants of the earth. There's no escape from his presence and expression. This declaration of his presence is recognised by young and old alike.

Some of the most magnificent hymns and majestic songs were inspired by the wonders of God's creative hand. Such inspiration thrills the human heart and transcends man's understanding, reinforcing the positiveness of his being.

Once man has been challenged to believe the reality of

God's existence, God will speak through his word, the Bible.

God's word

This is the most important way in which God speaks. The voice of the Lord will never contradict the Scriptures, and is never left to private interpretation. If God speaks, he is consistent with what he has already revealed as truth. His word, sharper than any two-edged sword, enables the believer to discern the difference between human thoughts and divine leading and uncovers hidden motivations and desires. The Christian who allows the word of Christ to dwell in him richly can distinguish the truth which God is speaking from the deceptions of the enemy and human desires.

In Mark 4:14–20, God's word is compared to seeds sown by a sower. These scriptural seeds, when sown in the proper soil, produce a remarkable harvest. Colossians 3:16 states that as the word of Christ mixed with wisdom dwells in the believer richly, then psalms, hymns and spiritual songs have an atmosphere in which to grow in the heart of the Christian. The phrase 'word of Christ' implies neither legalistic rules nor mere information. This 'word' refers to that revelation of the Word, Jesus, which is alive and real in the person's heart.

The most stable foundation for building the song of the Lord is the revelation of the abundant truth in the Scriptures. I find that frequently, as I study various Bible subjects, God will give me songs as these truths have become reality in my heart. It requires more than one brick to construct a foundation for a house if it is to be sufficiently supported. Likewise, the song of the Lord is established through the richness of the variety of the scriptural truths revealed to the heart. Songs born without such a foundation possess no substance and frequently result in doctrinal error, emotional outbursts and personal opinion. God's word, like a seed planted in the believer's heart, will produce psalms, hymns and spiritual songs, which teach and admonish the church. Another vital factor is the wisdom which must accompany the revelation of the word, in terms of timing, accuracy of delivery and the nature of the company in which the song is to be ministered.

The renewed mind plays an important role in the release of the song of the Lord. As a Christian develops and matures by feeding on the word of God, this will be reflected in the songs which he or she sings. The mature believer ministers the song of the Lord with a solid doctrinal and scriptural message and in a manner which emphasises wisdom and grace. No Christian should ever be allowed to minister outside of God's word. Continued growth depends on regular food. As newborn babies yearn and cry out for their milk, so the believer should continually desire God's word. This childlike attitude is mandatory, no matter how long you have known the Lord. The song of the Lord can grow stale when it's not constantly inspired with fresh manna from the word of God. As God speaks through his word, as the seeds of truth are planted deep within your heart and as you recognise his voice, songs will result for his glory.

The inward witness

The inward witness is another important way in which God speaks to the Christian: 'The Spirit Himself bears witness with our spirit that we are children of God' (Rom 8:16); 'I tell the truth in Christ, I am not lying, my conscience also bearing me witness in the Holy Spirit' (Rom 9:1); '. . . who show the work of the law written in their hearts, their conscience also bearing witness, and between themselves their thoughts accusing or else excusing them' (Rom 2:15). It is also the one which is most frequently ignored and reasoned away. This inward witness is best described as a deep-seated and persistent conviction, often called a 'gut feeling'. Actually, the inward witness is the voice of the human conscience which discerns the difference between right and wrong and urges the believer to choose what is right. Unbelievers also possess this inward witness but, unfortunately, may tend to describe it as 'being psychic'. However, the unbeliever's conscience is tainted by sin and by the self; it is ruled by Satan and not sanctified by the blood of Jesus. It is therefore an untrustworthy guide. But the conscience of the Christian who is Spirit-led and walking in the word is a most trustworthy source of help. The inward witness, through the leading of the Holy Spirit who indwells the believer, is one of the avenues through which God warns us of trouble and leads us into his perfect will for our lives.

The purpose of the inward witness in hearing the song of the Lord is to prompt us to prepare for the birth of a song and then to pray, so that the song is ministered suitably. I've been so grateful to God for his provision of this means of guidance, even when it didn't seem to make any natural sense.

My husband and I were in Sweden and I was speaking at a praise and worship conference in Gothenburg. Following the Saturday evening service, I was conscious of a strong prompting in my heart that the Lord wanted me to sing a certain song about the name of Jesus at the service on the following Sunday morning. The pastor of the church had already asked me if I'd sing at the service, but didn't say anything about the theme of his message. I kept trying to reason away this witness, arguing in my mind that since the song wasn't in Swedish, surely God wouldn't want it to be sung. Yet the prompting persisted; the witness was so strong I knew I didn't dare be disobedient, lest I grieve the Holy Spirit. So I sang the song as the Lord had directed. As I finished, I noticed the shock on the pastor's face. He was deeply moved. Why? The message for that morning's sermon was about the name of the Lord! I didn't know that by natural knowledge, but God knew.

Time and again, even before any words or melody are given, God will begin to prompt me with the knowledge that he's placed the seeds for a song in my heart and anointed me to deliver it at the appropriate time. The inward witness then stirs me to prayer and develops my sensitivity to the times and seasons of ministry. Sometimes I'll perceive in my heart that a song is going to be born twenty-four hours or even several days in advance. Ministry of the song of the Lord needs such sensitivity and preparation.

Yet the inward witness is not only valuable before the song is given. While actually ministering the song, I constantly stir myself to be sensitive as to whether I'm delivering it in the manner which the Spirit of God desires. The inward knowing assists us in determining if the listeners are able to receive the song. Jesus knew, for example, when the people reasoned in their hearts and were doubting his ministry (Mk 2:6–8).

The inward witness guides us in how the words should be enunciated and how the music is to be played, and the list goes on. Developing in the inward witness is a minute-by-minute, hour-by-hour, day-by-day process. In ministering the song of the Lord to others we must train ourselves to be sensitive to God's direction and leading.

The human conscience warns us when we are in danger of sin. Like a hazard warning light, the Spirit-inspired awareness sounds the alarm that we need in order to avoid and conquer sin. But this God-given tool is designed for one reason, and one reason alone: so that we can be pleasing to God and follow him in all we do. This applies to our daily life, our individual ministries and callings and the song of the Lord. Thank God for the inward witness!

The inward voice

Lying on my bed, I didn't want to get up. The previous day had been horrendous. The prospect of a glorious 'pity party' beckoned attractively. How easy it would be to feel sorry for myself! Wrapping up in the warm blankets I prepared to enjoy some selfish slumber. There was only one problem. In my heart I heard praise songs encouraging me to shout for joy and they sounded like a bugle call to arise and shine. Ugh! I was experiencing the struggle, which every Christian has known, between the Spirit within me and the carnal self.

Reluctantly, I forced myself out of my comfortable hideout and started to sing. The words didn't come with a tremendous amount of enthusiasm on my part, yet none the less I knew the best thing for me was to co-operate with the help of the Spirit of God. Singing the words of the songs as I heard them being sung in my heart, I felt the blanket of heaviness and sorrow begin to lift. A choice must be made. God doesn't need our help— he needs our co-operation. This was the case as I heard the inward voice; one of God's methods of speaking to the Christian.

The inward voice is the expression of God's Spirit as he speaks a word in the Christian's spirit over and over again. Some identify it as the still small voice. The inward voice of God's Spirit is more direct and tangible than the inward witness. The inward voice grants direction in times of need and ministry. 'Your ears shall hear a word behind you, saying, "This is the way, walk in it," whenever you turn to the right hand or whenever you turn to the left' (Is 30:21).

Philip the evangelist heard the Spirit of the Lord speak to him in such a way when he met the Ethiopian eunuch (Acts 8:26–30). The danger with this type of hearing is the possibility of deception and abuse. Christians are desperate to hear God. Unfortunately, instead of seeking him through his word, they chase after voices. This is dangerous. There are thousands of voices in the world and none of them is insignificant. Familiar spirits thrive on the desperation of Christians who will do anything to hear God, except study his word.

The inward voice is a helpful tool in ministering the song of the Lord. For example, as God speaks to the individual in this manner, songs of praise will seem almost to ring in the believer's mind and heart. This expression of the Lord's voice helps the Christian to sing a spiritual song, worshipping God in the Spirit through the vehicle of the human spirit. The purpose of these songs is to position the individual in a place of faith and praise. Remember the first priority of the song of the Lord is hearing his song to us and then singing it back to him!

The second stage is hearing by means of the inward voice songs of prophecy, new songs and psalms destined to be ministered to others. Also, when God speaks in this way, the song may take the form of a word of knowledge or wisdom. My experience is that God gives me these types of song piece by piece, phrase by phrase, melody by melody. Sometimes it may take months before the song is completed. But if God builds the house, or in this case the song, it will stand! I don't want to build a song by my efforts. The ministry of such songs demands sensitivity and discernment. In Acts 8, God instructed Philip in where, what and how. We must listen to God and wait for his timing and anointing.

Ministry gifts of the Spirit

On one occasion, I was reflecting on the theme of a sermon I'd just heard. The speaker had preached on Barnabas, the apostle of encouragement. Many times before I had considered the importance of Barnabas' role; we have already noted the significant part he played in encouraging and supporting the apostle Paul (Acts 9:27). How the church needs people like Barnabas today!

As I meditated on this, a song began to stir in my heart. God had used the preaching of the word to speak to me. Preaching (a form of prophecy) is only one of the ministry gifts of the Spirit which God may use in this way. Teaching, words of knowledge, words of wisdom and even the interpretation of tongues have also inspired many of the songs which the Lord has given me. We must learn to listen and to recognise, by the inward witness, when God is speaking to us through these ministry gifts. Thank God for the gifts of the Spirit!

Dreams

But no one says, 'Where is God my Maker, who gives songs in the night . . .?' (Job 35:10).

The Lord will command His loving kindness in the daytime, and in the night His song shall be with me—a prayer to the God of my life (Ps 42:8).

It was approximately 2:30 am. Lying beneath the bed-covers, I struggled to wake up. In a dream, I'd seen myself preaching at a conference at which I was in reality sched-uled to minister the following week. In the dream, I moved to the piano after finishing my sermon and began to sing a prophetic song to the pastors and ministers present. As I sang, they began to weep, and the glory of God manifested in the form of a cloud. Then I woke, with a sense of urgency pervading my soul. This song of the Lord must be written down, or I might lose it.

With the words and music still resounding in my heart, I forced myself out of bed, found a piece of paper and began to write down the words. 'Though my people stand in broken stones and rubble from the onslaught of an unseen evil foe, yet by my word I'll burn away the stubble, for I will restore my church. Some of you are called as Nehemiah, to rebuild the walls by the order of your King . . .' Each word seemed packed with power. Completing the text, I returned to the warm covers of my bed. Now fully awake, I lay there and trembled at the message of the song and sermon which I knew I was called to give the following week.

One week later, after speaking the message I'd heard in the dream, I sat down at the piano and began to play the 'Nehemiah song'. Men and women began to kneel, lift their hands and weep as God's glory rolled into the room, and I thanked God for his song. He knows how to speak in a way that will be suitable to our needs. He is the God who gives songs in the night. One of the ways he does this is through dreams.

The Lord speaks through dreams in various situations. Both the unsaved and the saved may have such dreams. God spoke to Joseph, Mary's espoused, in a dream. Through a dream, God also spoke to Pharaoh, king of

Egypt, who was an idolatrous heathen. But not all dreams are from God. The prophets of Baal had false dreams. Many dreams are simply the result of an over-active imagination. However, when God chooses to speak through a dream, it makes such a dramatic impact upon the heart that fearful wonder may result.

Through dreams God spoke to individuals about their finances, their safety and their future. He gave them guidance and chastened them to repentance. Symbols, shadows and types are common means of expression in dreams, but are often misunderstood and over-emphasised. However, when God gives a song in the night through a dream, the words and melody are like a fire branded into the heart. However, human memory is not infallible, so if God gives such a song I believe it's important to write it down as soon as I wake up.

The Scriptures will either prove or disprove the authenticity of songs given in the night. Any spiritual song which stirs the soul, leads the individual to pray and is confirmed by God's word is probably from the Lord. On the other hand, songs which produce fear and introspection rather than peace, faith and love; which harm the believer's relationship with God and other Christians aren't genuine songs of the Lord. When receiving the 'Nehemiah song', I knew from Bible study that the song was doctrinally and scripturally accurate. Test everything according to the full counsel of God's word.

Some dreams, like Joseph's dream of the stars and the moon bowing to the sun, will not be fulfilled until many years later. Store those dreams away until the appropriate time and situation arrive. There's a time to speak and a time to stay silent. One safe principle to apply whenever we feel God has spoken to us, in any way, is found in

James: 'So then, my beloved brethren, let every man be swift to hear, slow to speak, slow to wrath' (Jas 1:19).

Visions

> Now the Lord spoke to Paul in the night by a vision, 'Do not be afraid, but speak, and do not keep silent' (Acts 18:9).

> Now there was a certain disciple at Damascus named Ananias; and to him the Lord said in a vision, 'Ananias.' And he said, 'Here I am, Lord' (Acts 9:10).

He walked into the Bible school classroom appearing rushed, tired and frustrated. It was Tuesday morning and the chapel service had already begun. Finding his chair, he slipped his books onto the table and promptly laid his head down upon his folded arms, preparing his heart.

Sitting at the piano, leading the class into praise and worship, I was particularly aware of the strong anointing of God's Spirit in the room. This was my second day with the class and I wondered what God had in store for us this morning. The Lord had moved so mightily through prophetic song the morning before. As the Spirit of God moved in healing, calling the students to know him, every person in the room had prostrated themselves upon the floor weeping, overwhelmed by his awesome presence. I didn't know what to expect this morning. Revival seemed to be at the door and I hoped we would know how to answer when the Spirit of God knocked.

Suddenly, after I had ministered praise and worship, as well as three or four songs of deliverance, my eyes were opened to see a vision that inspired a song. This song of the Lord would minister to the weary young man in the class.

In my vision I saw so many faces it was impossible to count them. They were the faces of young people from all races, all desperate for help, needing Christ. They formed a huge mass of young humanity, continually increasing in number. The vision was startlingly clear; the message evident. This weary young man was called by God. He had a vision for young people that would bring the reality of Christ into the lives of thousands. Through this ministry the nations would be touched as these young people shared the gospel of Jesus.

I began to sing about the vision as the words for the song bubbled up in my heart. The young man, named Tom, began to sob. He fell to his knees, then lay face down on the floor. Every few minutes he would return to his chair and begin to write furiously, recording the words God was speaking to his heart. Back and forth he went between the floor and the table, constantly weeping, constantly rejoicing.

After chapel, I was informed that this young man was a youth pastor, called and zealous for God. The vision which had inspired the song was the very same vision for the ministry which he had received from the Lord some time before. Through the song, God had confirmed to him his calling, his heartfelt burden and the reality of his mission. This song was one of those which leave an indelible mark.

Visions are another tool through which God speaks. But they may be misunderstood, misinterpreted and often misused in the corporate assembly of God's people. Through true visions, God powerfully communicates with the individual believer and with the church. But the subject must be properly understood, or great harm can result. We must learn to distinguish clearly between the products of the imagination and revelations genuinely inspired by the Holy Spirit. The criterion for judging anything which purports to be a vision must be God's word.

There are in fact several types of vision illustrated in Scripture. Let's look at them in detail.

The open vision. Open visions are the least common type of vision (see 1 Samuel 3:1). In an open vision, the believer's natural eyes are opened as well as their spiritual eyes. The things of the spiritual realm are clearly seen among natural phenomena. These visions occur infrequently and generally in times of extreme need or danger, or in prophetic times.

Trances. In a trance, the believer's physical senses are temporarily suspended and the person is only conscious of seeing the things of the Spirit. Acts 10:9–16 relates how Peter, while in prayer, fell into a trance in which God rebuked him concerning his wrong attitude towards the Gentiles. Sometimes I wonder whether God uses a trance to shake believers out of an ungodly manner of behaviour. No matter what the reason, a vision in a trance is bound to get your attention. I have described in a previous chapter my experience of seeing the throne room of heaven and hearing the masses sing 'Worthy is the Lamb'. In that moment, I fell into a trance. Temporarily I was more conscious of the realm of God's Spirit than of my present surroundings. This hasn't happened regularly, and I don't base my relationship with Jesus on the frequency or lack of these experiences. Nevertheless, we can't ignore the fact that they do exist.

Night visions. Night visions, similar to dreams, are those manifestations of God's Spirit in which God speaks during the night. These night visions most frequently occurred in times of extreme duress. Daniel, Joseph, David and Jacob experienced such night visions.

Seeing in the spirit. This is perhaps the commonest form of vision. Probably the easiest way to define 'seeing in the spirit' is to compare it to the rapid flash of a small slide photo on a white screen in a darkened room. Though momentary, the picture is very real. However, this type of vision is particularly likely to be misunderstood and misused, owing to the partial knowledge it conveys. Great wisdom and self-control must be exercised before ministering this form of revelation, otherwise confusion will inevitably result. These visions or spiritual flashes are like single pieces of a puzzle. If we'll be patient, pray and search his word, he will grant us more pieces to the puzzle. The Christian needs to be more concerned about the wisdom with which this type of vision is delivered than with the actual vision itself. God will never rebuke you for seeking his timing, his knowledge, more under-standing and loving sensitivity in ministering a vision from heaven. Remember, we must be swift to hear and slow to speak. Frequently we learn these things the hard way. But wisdom should never be tossed out of the window in the zeal of the moment. The anointing always waits for wisdom. God isn't the God of confusion—he's the God of peace.

I will give an example from my own experience. I was leading a series of classes and at the praise and worship service on the Monday morning my attention was drawn to an older couple on the front row. Despite the awesome presence of God which filled the room, their hearts seemed heavy. As I led the group in singing, I made a mental note to spend some extra time in prayer for them.

Perhaps God would minister to them before the week's classes were over. Suddenly, as I looked towards this couple, I saw a momentary flash on my 'spirit screen'. A young man, wayward and far from God, was about to make a choice for the Lord and comfort the heart of his parents. My heart thrilled and rejoiced for them. Oh, how they'd be encouraged! A song began to bubble up in my heart for them as I reflected on the revelation. Yet as I observed their brokenness of spirit, I sensed the war of unbelief raging against their souls. I knew then that if I was to minister this word in song at that moment, the words would fall upon the unprepared soil of their hearts. The song would have to wait. My heart ached for them, yet timing was of the essence if they were to be ministered to. Perhaps tomorrow. Tuesday's praise and worship service came and went; the time was still not right. Wednesday was the same. Would God release me or was this song reserved for another time altogether? Finally, on Thursday morning, I saw the beginnings of faith sparkling in their eyes. Again the picture came, clear as the first time I saw it. But now, in an atmosphere of faith, they were ready to receive it. Weeping, they fell onto each other's shoulders, shaking under the power of God's loving hand. Miraculously he healed them. Through one picture, wisely timed and prayerfully ministered, this couple was set free.

Before leaving the subject of visions, it is important that we should recognise the fact that there are such things as false visions.

False visions. False visions may resemble genuine visions but are actually either demonic or—most often—soulish in nature. Their origin is clearly explained in Scripture. It is impossible here to deal with this subject in any depth but I do want to attempt some description of how false visions can be distinguished from true, since unfortunately discernment in this area is sometimes lacking.

The prophets of Baal and other false prophets mentioned in Scripture were instruments of the enemy, delivering false visions to the people of God. In the church today, false visions are more often produced by the uncontrolled imaginations of people whose desire to hear God, or be used by him, is either untempered by wisdom or lacking in humility. Such visions are inspired by human emotions and desires. They may either promise enormous blessings corresponding to the individual's hopes or foretell unrelieved doom and judgement which reflect his critical spirit. There is seldom a balance in these visions; doom and judgement are not accompanied by the hope of mercy nor the promise of prosperity with exhortation to live a godly life.

False visions are also characterised by vagueness and obscurity and may take the form of nonsensical and irrelevant pictures. These may be offered by people with sincere hearts but if they are accepted as genuine they leave behind a trail of confusion. This is especially so if they are given in the corporate gathering. Depending on their attitude of heart, those who communicate such visions in the corporate gathering may either express puzzlement as to the meaning of the picture or, in an attempt to appear spiritual, try to force an interpretation. In either case, confusion results. Although it is true that we prophesy in part, this cannot be held to excuse the sort of vagueness we are discussing here.

However impressive a vision may appear, it is imperative that we test it; false visions manipulate the hopes and fears of innocent and immature Christians. The full counsel of God's word is a trustworthy standard by which to judge. And if a vision brings confusion, we can be sure that it's not from God.

These, then, are the seven primary ways in which God speaks. He may also speak to us through other people, such as parents or ministers, or through our circumstances. On rare occasions he may speak audibly or by an angel, though this is likely only in extremely difficult or painful circumstances.

Hindrances to hearing the Lord's song and voice

If our ability to sing the song of the Lord depends on our first hearing him, we must at all times take care to deal with anything which might keep us from hearing clearly. The following are the commonest hindrances.

Unbelief

At the very beginning of this chapter we saw that to deny that God is speaking is to contradict his word. Please may I emphasise again that repentance is the only way to remove this hindrance. Without this change of heart the believer will never learn to recognise God's voice when he speaks.

A sense of inadequacy

Many Christians feel that inadequacies in certain areas make them unable to receive and transmit a word from the Lord. Moses expressed such a fear—and God rebuked him (Exod 4:10–14). We must not allow the perception of our weaknesses and our fear of failure to become an excuse for not hearing from God. Shyness, lack of education, age and gender have all been offered as excuses; but what God requires is a committed heart. He made our mouths and he can fill them, as Moses subsequently discovered when he received from the Lord the song of witness which we have already studied. Remember that the Lord is the One who gives the tongue of the learned (Is 50:4).

The condition of the conscience

We saw earlier that the conscience plays a tremendous role in hearing the voice of the Lord, especially in the area of the inward witness. But consciousness of sin makes the believer reluctant to seek the presence of God. We must always strive therefore, like St Paul, to lead a godly life and have a 'conscience without offence towards God and men' (Acts 24:16). And if we fail, we must not despair: through the blood of Jesus we *can* 'draw near with a true heart in full assurance of faith, having our hearts sprinkled from an evil conscience' (Heb 10:22). If we confess our sin, he forgives and our relationship is restored so that we can hear his voice once more.

Distractions

Distractions overwhelm the heart and steal away the assurance that God will indeed speak. They choke the seed of God's word, like thorns (see Mark 4:18–19). The cares of this world, the deceitfulness of riches and desires for other things are formidable hindrances.

Lack of trust

When God speaks we must respond in faith. God spoke to the Hebrew children, but the word 'did not profit them, not being mixed with faith in those who heard it' (Heb 4:2). God doesn't always tell us everything at once. He waits for us to respond in obedient faith to what he has already told us, before speaking to us further. I know this from experience. Often, I have no more than two or three words before I am called to minister the song of the Lord. But I know his voice and that I can trust him to fill my mouth; that if I obey, he will give me more.

17

Edification Is the Goal

We have looked at the various categories of the song of the Lord and the ways in which they function in the life of the individual and in the life of the church. We have also noted that the person who wishes to minister the song of the Lord must observe certain guidelines and scriptural principles if he or she is to sing in a way which is pleasing to God. I think it will be helpful at this point to give a brief summary of these guidelines and principles.

The first and indispensable principle is that before you can sing the song of the Lord you must first hear his song and his voice speaking to you. This means that you must spend time with him on a regular basis; a daily devotional time with the Lord is essential. Only thus will you have a right relationship with him and be in a position of faith and praise in which your own songs of praise to him will be born. There are some songs of the Lord which are only to be sung within the context of the individual's private devotional times.

The individual will also receive from the Lord songs which are to be ministered to others, including the corporate gathering. These songs too are born out of a personal relationship with God: it is in his presence that the seed of the song of the Lord is planted. If you lack a relationship with God, any attempt to minister to others will be empty. And if your personal spiritual needs are not being met by spending time alone with him, you may be tempted to satisfy them by means of ministering the song of the Lord in public, which is selfish. This brings us to another vital principle concerning songs of the Lord which are delivered in the corporate gathering.

Edifying the body of Christ

When ministered in public, the gift of the song of the Lord, like all spiritual gifts, has as its goal the edification of the body. We are all members of the body of Christ and everything we do and everything we are affects the other members for good or ill. We have therefore a great responsibility to ensure that what we minister, and the way in which we minister it, will build up the body rather than damage it. Paul told the Corinthian church that the prior condition of ministering spiritual gifts is to pursue the 'more excellent way' of love (1 Cor 12:31–14:1). Without love, the song of the Lord is no more than a clanging cymbal. If we love our fellow members in the body of Christ and wish to edify them, our ministry will be governed by the following principles.

A prepared heart and song

Only a song that is truly from the Lord will edify, which is why, as I said above, it is essential to spend time with the Lord in order to receive songs from him. Don't make the mistake of thinking that 'spontaneous' always means 'spiritual'; sometimes this isn't the case. Remember also that the song of the Lord must have a biblical foundation and contain a solid, doctrinal, scriptural message. All songs should be tested by scriptural standards.

The heart must be prepared as well as the song. What is in the heart comes out in the delivery of the song; if the heart is affected by strife, bitterness or depression, this will be communicated to the hearer. Prepare your heart so as to minister love and grace. Ephesians 4:29 says that our words should impart grace, in order to edify.

Examine your motives

The foundational criterion here is whether you are seeking to minister the song of the Lord for the sake of the group or for your own sake. Where love towards others is not the governing principle there is always the temptation to promote the self and satisfy personal needs and desires. The song of the Lord should never be used as a way of parading one's spirituality, boosting one's self-esteem or impressing others. Motives such as these lead to competitiveness and disregard for the ministry of others. All these things are entirely contrary to Paul's teaching about love in 1 Corinthians 13. Love does not parade itself; does not seek its own; does not behave rudely.

Don't allow wrong motives to lead you into envy of another person's gift. Remember that, like every Christian, you are unique and so is your gifting. All our gifts are given by the will of the Holy Spirit so we should use the gift he has given us rather than try to exercise a different gift.

Examining our motives is important because it enables us to distinguish a strong personal desire to minister from true God-given zeal.

Ministering within wise boundaries

Sensitivity in choosing the appropriate time and the most constructive manner of delivery will lead to edification through the song of the Lord. This requires the exercise of self-discipline. The matter of preparation is again important here; lack of preparation can produce a tendency to yield to impulses and a failure to exercise self-discipline.

Musical accompaniment should also be sensitive and appropriate. Perhaps I should say at this point that the song of the Lord does not depend on a high level of musical knowledge. However, such knowledge can greatly assist the development and release of the song, if it is properly used. It should not become restrictive and should operate within the freedom of God's grace.

Church leaders have a vital role to play. The ministry offices of apostle, prophet, evangelist, pastor and teacher were given for the edifying of the body of Christ. Wise and godly leadership promotes and facilitates the ministry of the song of the Lord by determining what is edifying and establishing appropriate scriptural boundaries. Such oversight prevents confusion and ensures that all things are done 'decently and in order' (1 Cor 14:40). 'Decently' means 'in a graceful and becoming way'; it suggests behaviour which is noble and honourable, as if presenting a gift to royalty. 'In order' implies that all things have their appointed place within a pattern. In the narrative in 1 Chronicles of the transporting of the Ark we saw how important it is to seek God's order and how the wise leadership of David and Chenaniah implemented this order. The boundaries set in place by wise leaders are beneficial and are not inimical to liberty. Liberty is given to us for service, not as a cloak for selfish motives and conduct.

The New Testament ministry of the praise and worship leader is one of helping rather than of authority and vision. Vision and direction come from the church leaders. Much conflict could be avoided if church leaders always took care to communicate their vision for the ministry of the song of the Lord to the praise and worship leaders. Church leaders should also seek to exercise their authority sensitively, and with humility bearing in mind the needs of their congregation, if they are to release rather than stifle the song of the Lord.

If you are present at a corporate gathering other than the one of which you are a member, remember that because of differences in church government and ministerial structure, churches differ as to what they allow and expect concerning the song of the Lord. Other churches may have guidelines and boundaries which differ from those of your own congregation. Some churches are not open to individual lay ministry of the song of the Lord, while others allow it with proper supervision and assistance. We should be sensitive about this and respect the appointed order of each church.

Finally, the size of the congregation will also determine what is edifying. In very large gatherings (upwards of several hundreds), the song of the Lord is best reserved for recognised leaders or those designated by them. This is because the difficulty of testing the song and the motives of the singer increases in proportion to the size of the gathering. The more intimate atmosphere of smaller groups affords opportunity for a larger number of people to minister and for the song of the Lord to develop. Both kinds of gathering have their peculiar advantages and problems.

If these principles are observed, the song of the Lord will edify the body. All of this requires a high degree of commitment, but God will strengthen us and enable us to meet the challenge. If other people make mistakes and minister unwisely, we should not heap criticism on them; rather, we should love them and pray for them. Let's grow in grace towards each other. True zeal, humility and love are the foundation of the song of the Lord.

18

You Can Sing the Song of the Lord

A potentially inexhaustible reservoir of spiritual songs remains untapped because thousands and thousands of Christians have believed a lie designed by Satan to silence the songs of the Lord for ever. But as the Spirit of the Lord brings into fulfilment the restoration of all things, this plot of darkness will be uncovered and the believer will once again realise what Philippians 4:13 truly means: 'I can do all things through Christ who strengthens me.' God delights in the liberty his children find when they begin to believe in the truth of this scripture. You can sing the song of the Lord. You have the potential within you. There is a sense in which you already possess everything you will ever receive from God. The works and songs which God intends you to minister have been prepared from the foundation of the world. We must learn to walk in those preordained steps by grace. Will you continue to allow the enemy to steal these gifts from you in exchange for fear of failure and rebuke? Heaven's host is watching and waiting for someone who will dare to believe in the Spirit who indwells them. You really can do it! Now will you try?

Consider how children learn to walk. They often fall, but seem to be indestructible, constantly bouncing back like rubber and trying again and again. Would you be walking today if as a child you had allowed the fear of failure to ground you? Singing the song of the Lord is much like learning to walk and talk. No one is able to run or talk fluently when they are just learning how. But if we step out in faith, even if we tumble we can bounce back and try again until we've learned. If you're willing to deal with these attitudes and believe in the One who lives in you, then you are ready to take the first steps and sing!

In this final chapter I will present a step-by-step plan for singing the song of the Lord. It may seem a little complex at first, but it really isn't that difficult once you've identified your heart and motives.

Taking the first steps

Step one: Define your motives and take any ungodly attitudes to the cross

This first step is extremely personal. Take an honest look at your relationship with the Lord. Ask yourself why you want to sing the Lord's song. What are the motives in your heart? Realise that any deception in this area must be exposed and confronted with the truth. Selfish ambition, proud deceptions and emotions and feelings contrary to the truth of the word of God must be nailed to the cross of Calvary. Protect yourself against the enemy both by acknowledging that you are susceptible to deception and by claiming your God-given ability to hear the truth. Remember that your first priority in singing the song of the Lord is being released to sing to him! Ministering to the Lord is one of the highest callings the Christian can possess.

Whether you are alone or in a group, this first step is by far the most important. Here are some suggestions to assist you in stepping out.

On nearly every occasion when I am instructing people in learning to sing the Lord's song, I find that one of the first ways of demonstrating a prepared heart is the lifting of the hands as a sign of being yielded to the Spirit of the Lord. The action implies a sense of dependence, submission, repentance, supplication and release to the Spirit. It is most profitable, for both individuals and groups who are longing to grow in the ministry of the Lord's song, to lift the hands with these attitudes in mind.

As the hands are lifted I will frequently lead the believers in a prayer of repentance for any wrong motives and any sin which could pervert the reception of the song. I still do this myself if I find that my heart has grown dull and hard of hearing. As hands are lifted in release, forgiveness is received in faith. Some believers simply need to say, 'I release these attitudes and sins at the cross. I receive the cleansing blood of Jesus and forgiveness for these things.'

Finally I ask people to commit themselves anew to loving God. Sometimes I may lead them in a simple worship chorus for the purpose of stimulating the love relationship. If a chorus *is* used, may I emphasise that it should be as simple and short as possible; it's best not to complicate this preparation.

Step two: Prepare an atmosphere of commitment, activate your will and express your faith

The psalmist David repeatedly illustrates this step. Committing himself in faith, he frequently used such phrases as 'I will bless the Lord', 'I will praise the Lord', and 'I will sing unto the Lord'. Many believers earnestly desire to sing the song of the Lord but don't believe that they can actually do it. Thousands of songs die in the desire stage because of failure to activate the will by faith.

In order to motivate the heart to receive, the believer must verbally state the faith in his or her heart for receiving the songs.

This is done by means of a prayer such as the one set out below. Please also keep in mind that in praying this prayer and making the following declarations, it is imperative that you believe what you are saying. Otherwise, this prayer will only be a ritual, and great disappointment will follow.

'Dear Lord, you promised that if the Hebrew children opened their mouths, you would fill them. I come to you as one of your children and at this moment I open my mouth to receive the words for the songs you desire to give me. You alone give the tongue of the learned. Open my ears, eyes and heart in Jesus' name, for my desire is to sing to you and to receive your song to me. Therefore, as an act of my will, and as the desire of my heart, I make the following declaration. I will sing unto the Lord new songs of praise and worship and inspired songs born of the Spirit. I will hear your song for me and I will sing to you of my faith and love for you. At this moment I receive by faith the inspiration, anointing, words and melodies for these songs. I thank you for them now. In Jesus' name. Amen!'

Often, as individuals and groups pray this prayer, a well of tears seems to burst open. Tears are not always a sign of spiritual breakthrough, but they are an indicator that the heart is beginning to open. Don't be afraid if such emotions rush to the surface while praying this prayer of commitment. God is at work in you and you can trust him to lead you.

In some situations, when working with groups, I find it is extremely helpful to ask the individuals to pray together that each other's ears, eyes and hearts may be opened. This will bring great blessing to all.

This step has been very important to me as I've prepared to minister in churches, or in my quiet times when I simply long to sing to the Lord and allow him to sing back to me. There have been innumerable times when my heart felt as dry as a desert and the well within me seemed devoid of any life. But when I have verbally declared my faith and will to sing to the Lord, he has always sovereignly met me, refreshing my heart and filling my mouth with good things. Even in those dry, wilderness periods of life, he is still faithful to sing his song!

Step three: Bring your thoughts and imaginations into subjection to the word of the Lord. Meditate on the things that God has done for you that you are thankful for

Like an untamed wild horse, our imaginations, thoughts and emotions are by far the most impetuous part of our nature and must be brought into subjection to God's word and Spirit if we are to go forward in the Lord's song.

You can begin taking this step by verbally announcing to yourself that you're decisively taking authority over your own thoughts, imagination and emotions, and bringing them into subjection to the word of God, the Spirit of God and the blood of Jesus. In doing this you've begun to close the door on the enemy's influence. This step is by far the most frustrating, because the longer you've been passive in this area, the greater the struggle will be, and the more runaway your thought-life. Don't give up. It will take some time and discipline. The benefits of your godly efforts will far outweigh the difficulties. It's also during this time that any hidden roots of rejection, inferiority and worthlessness will attempt to thwart your efforts to obey. Negative emotions are real—but this does not mean they are necessarily the truth. The truth is determined by what God's word says and our feelings, however real, must be submitted to this truth. We are not required to deny our emotions but to choose to believe God's word rather than what we feel. Fight these thoughts and feelings with the promises of the Scriptures. When dealing with feelings of rejection, use such scriptures as, 'I have been made accepted in the beloved.' Find the appropriate truth and cast down any runaway thoughts. Allow the word of God to renew your mind.

Secondly, your thoughts must be disciplined by fixing your mind upon the things which you're thankful for. Consciously recall these things. Identifying what we are thankful for is the seedbed of the new song of praise—a primary and mandatory step if we are ever to develop in the other types of the song of the Lord.

While ministering to one particular international gathering of praise and worship leaders I had led them through preparation steps one and two, and had begun to deal with step three. Up to that point everything had gone like clockwork. But as I prepared to lead them on it was as though I had hit an impenetrable brick wall. As I listened to their prayers I realised that in this group of leaders all emotion and heartfelt feeling was repressed by an intellectualisation of praise and worship. Their hearts were so dominated by their reasoning that they didn't know how to cast down their thoughts and imagination. It was as though their hearts were miles away from their heads. I knew that the Holy Spirit within them had to be released or we would remain in this dead-lock situation. The key to this release was the verbal expression of *heartfelt* testimonies of thankfulness. As these believers began to share with one another some fresh testimonies of how the Lord had worked in their lives, the lid was taken off the well of their hearts. A few minutes spent quietly meditating on all God has done for you will stir up thankfulness in your heart; then as you speak it out, to yourself and to others, it will increase and God has something to work with.

Remember, as you activate your will and subject your mind to the Spirit and the word, you will bring your mind and your will into co-operation with his will. But this doesn't mean you are not supposed to think. God doesn't need zombies. Discipline your thoughts and keep your spirit and your mind connected at all times. Let me give you an example in this principle.

On one occasion, during a series of revival meetings, I received a song from the Lord, based on Psalm 45:7. I began to minister the song to the congregation and encouraged them to join me in it. When we had been singing for a while, I noticed my husband frantically trying to attract my attention. Unaware of how tired I had become, I hadn't noticed that instead of singing 'I hate wickedness and I love righteousness' I had begun to sing 'I love wickedness and I hate righteousness'. I stopped singing and explained to the congregation what had happened. Fortunately, they were understanding and we were able to laugh at the things that happen when, perhaps through tiredness, our spirit and our mind disconnect.

Step four: Sing familiar choruses of joyful praise. Stir up the joy! Sing in the spirit, sing in understanding. Sing from the sweetness of your heart

As you are quietly praying, begin to sing songs of joy; sing choruses of praise which are familiar, but make room for new words to bubble up in your heart to the Lord. I would also encourage you, if you've received the gift of tongues, to use that gift and sing in the spirit with melodies both familiar and new. I've observed that often we seem to prefer to sing only the songs our mind intellectually understands and ignore the importance of singing from our spirit in co-operation with the Holy Spirit. The songs of the Spirit are born out of the reality of 'heart knowledge' and cannot be replaced by intellectual endeavours. The depths of God's Spirit are only touched as we extend ourselves from the depths of our hearts.

Step five: Quiet your heart and ask the Lord for a single phrase and sing it to a familiar melody or a new melody as you have freedom. Apply favourite scriptures to familiar melodies or new melodies

When your heart is quiet, ask the Lord to give you a single phrase. If necessary, sing that phrase to a melody which you already know. If you're finding all this extremely difficult, then choose a favourite Scripture verse and apply a melody to this, remembering to take every runaway thought captive while concentrating on the words of these verses. Gradually, open your heart bit by bit, choosing each thought and word carefully; refuse every thought, word and emotion which is contrary to God's word, to God's nature and to faith and love. If at any time condemnation or frustration should arise, cast those thoughts down and return to the familiar choruses of praise. The more quickly we learn to relax in this attitude of heart, the more readily we will hear his words and leading without extreme complication.

At a family camp once in the United States, I gave a workshop on the prophetic song. After I had led a group of believers through the steps necessary to receive the songs of the Lord, I prepared them to sing simple phrases of praise to the melody of a familiar chorus. For a few very long minutes, they sat in absolute silence, hesitant to take the first step of faith and sing out a simple phrase. Finally one brave soul ventured out into the spiritual waters and sang. After this, a few more moments passed before someone else stepped out in faith. Slowly but genuinely, one after another they began to sing. The phrases started out so simple, but before the session was complete, beautiful poetical songs were born in praise, prophecy and worship. It reminded me of how popcorn pops. It starts out slowly, but once the oil is hot more and more kernels burst into tender popcorn. It was a wonderful time for all, and the most beautiful aspect of it was the sweet and tangible presence of the glory of the Lord.

In stepping out and making those first attempts, be willing to make wrong decisions and mistakes, because you will make them, as we all do at some time. Your aim is to unlock your heart to sing a new song to the Lord. Let him give you the words, making room for him to do so according to the truth of the word and the leading of the Spirit. Don't allow yourself to get frustrated if you're not immediately fluent in ministering the song of the Lord in the corporate setting. *The individual expression of the Lord's song in your personal devotions is the most important song of the Lord of all.* Keep in mind that all believers have been granted different graces, talents, spiritual abilities and proportions of faith. Be satisfied to function according to the grace God has given you and grow in that.

A sign of the Last Days

The Last Days believer is about to see a tremendous prophecy fulfilled. Many years have passed since the Lord's song has been heard in the way in which it's about to be released in the earth once again. Out of the wilderness God's people will soon emerge singing his song anew. The tongue of the dumb, once restrained, will be loosed. The rivers of the Spirit will flow and the parched land of human souls will be refreshed.

> The wilderness and the wasteland shall be glad for them, and the desert shall rejoice and blossom as the rose; it shall blossom abundantly and rejoice, even with joy and singing. The glory of Lebanon shall be given to it, the excellence of Carmel and Sharon. They shall see the glory of the Lord, the excellency of our God. Strengthen the weak hands, and make firm the feeble knees. Say to those who are fearful-hearted, 'Be strong, do not fear! Behold, your God will come with vengeance, with the recompense of God; He will come and save you.' Then the eyes of the blind shall be opened, and the ears of the deaf shall be unstopped. Then the lame shall leap like a deer, and the tongue of the dumb sing. For waters shall burst forth in the wilderness, and streams in the desert. The parched ground shall become a pool, and the thirsty land springs of water; in the habitation of jackals, where each lay, there shall be grass with reeds and rushes (Is 35:1–7).

Perhaps we shall experience a divine visitation similar to that granted to the deaf and dumb man in Mark 7. Away from the presence and distractions of the multitude, Jesus ministered to the afflicted man, commanding his ears to be opened. Immediately, there in that isolated spot, the man's hearing was restored and his tongue was loosed.

Jesus, the Lord of the song, will once again visit his people. He alone can and will open the deafened ears and loose the stilled tongues. But until we're willing to come away from the multitudes and meet with him one to one, our ears will remain closed and our tongues will remain silent. The time has indeed come for the believer to meet him face to face. As we wait upon him, in the shadow of his wings, he will restore the sound of his voice to our ears and the melody of his song to our mouths. No longer will we need to wonder if we can sing the song of the Lord in this foreign land we call earth. We can sing the songs of Zion in a strange land. Babylon will no longer take captive the song of the Lord. In this final hour, his song will be heard once again in the earth, but only after we've sought to sing the song to him first. Heal your church, Lord! May this cry be our united prayer. Let the ears of your people be opened and the tongues of your people be loosed again to sing the songs of Zion before you return!

Glossary

Altaschith Destroy or corrupt not. Probably the opening words of a popular song.

Anah To answer or respond in singing.

Babylon Babylon was once a great capital city of the Chaldean empire, located in present-day Iraq and ruled by some of the most idolatrous, wicked kings ever to reign on the earth. A major economic and religious centre of the world at that time, possessing vast wealth and resources, it became also a centre for music. Babylon is known in Scripture as 'mother of harlots'. Its song will be seductive and enticing to the flesh. Its name means 'confusion'. It was the conqueror of the tribe of Judah, or 'praise'. It is also the end-times enemy of the church.

Biyn The definition embraces the concepts of understanding, insight and discernment. To be skilful, cunning, intelligent, discerning, sensible, prudent, eloquent.

Chadash Something new or fresh.

Chenaniah The individual responsible for leading and overseeing the procession of Levites and priests as they carried the Ark of the Covenant to Jerusalem. His name means 'planted' or 'established by Jehovah'.

Giyl To turn and spin round in circles as if under the influence of violent emotion. *Giyl* is an extremely common word used for rejoicing and joy.

Judah The name of the fourth son of Jacob and the founder of a tribal family. The name means 'praise' and is compared to a plough in Hosea 10:11.

Massa The burden of a prophecy or song, the weight of which is great due to the responsibility required to deliver it properly.

Michtam An engraving, or a poem which by implication inscribes an indelible mark. Some translate the word as 'a golden poem'. The exact meaning is not known.

Ranan To creak or emit a stridulous sound; to shout (usually for joy); to rejoice; to cry out for joy; to sing aloud for joy and triumph.

Rinnah Loud crying or singing; a creaking or shrill sound of joy or grief; a cry of gladness, joy, proclamation, rejoicing.

Ron A loud cry or song; a shout of deliverance.

School of the prophets A group and gathering of individuals desirous to be used in prophecy would gather round those individuals called as prophets to be trained in the prophetic ministry.

Seer Most scholars agree that the term seer is synonymous with prophet—someone who sees into things that are normally hidden and hears things that are normally beyond the human ear.

Shemenith The eighth, the octave. Probably an eight-stringed instrument or lyre. Carries the idea of plumpness. Eight is a cardinal number, as if a surplus above the perfect number seven. The root words carry the idea of richness, plenty, fat, with the symbolic meaning of richness in anointing.

Shiggiaion or *Shigionoth* A poem that rambles and is set to wild, ecstatic wandering rhythms and corresponding music.

Shir The idea of a strolling minstrelsy.

Simchah Joy and rejoicing; bright, cheerful, joyful and glad.

Song of the Lord A song born out of the believer's right relationship with God, originating in his song as it already is in the heart and sung out at the appropriate time as led and anointed by the Spirit. It is often prophetic and prayer-orientated, and can either be prepared or spontaneous. It is scriptural in context and produces a deep and lasting effect in the heart of the singer and the hearer.

Songs of Ascents The songs which were sung by pilgrims travelling to Zion.

Suws To be bright and cheerful; to rejoice.

Tephillah A prayer which is most probably sung as part of formal worship.

Uzzah The son of Abinadab who died from touching the Ark of the Covenant while it was being transported to Jerusalem. His name means 'strength'.

Yacar To chastise, admonish, correct, instruct, discipline. The instruction corrects and guides singers into an orderly fashion of ministry.

Bibliography

Coleman, William L. *Today's Handbook of Bible Times and Customs.*

Conner, Kevin. *The Tabernacle of David.*

Freeman, James M. *Manners and Customs of the Bible.*
The International Standard Bible Encyclopedia Vols 1–4.

Josephus. *The Works.*

Lockyer, Herbert. *All the Men of the Bible.*
All the Trades and Occupations of the Bible.
All the Women of the Bible.

Soltau. *The Tabernacle.*

Strong's *Exhaustive Concordance of the Bible.*

Young's *Analytical Concordance of the Bible.*

Trombley, Charles. *Praise: Faith in Action.*

Vine's *Expository Dictionary of New Testament Words.*

Zodhiates, Spiros. *The Hebrew/Greek Key Study Bible.*